KON VS. MIYAZAKI

Michael Andre-Driussi

Sirius Fiction

To Dr. Sumie Jones, for providing the opportunities for me to lecture, and for comments upon this book.

CONTENTS

INTRODUCTION

So I drew you in with a catchy title? Thank you for being here.

This is a volume of essays, reviews, and lectures starting in 2005. It begins with Hayao Miyazaki, whose films first enchanted me in 1997. A few years later I discovered Satoshi Kon and began writing and lecturing about his work as well.

In the course of these many years, as I thought about both directors' work, the idea that Kon was responding to Miyazaki began percolating. You'll see the result in the last section. Enjoy!

Spoiler Warnings
Miyazaki Won an Oscar—Spoiler free
Four Miyazaki Points—Spoilers for *Castle in the Sky*
Kiki's Text into Film—Spoilers for *Kiki's Delivery Service*
Kiki's Italian Model—Spoilers for *Kiki's Delivery Service* and Pietrangeli's *I Knew Her Well*
Mononoke: the Dark Side of Miyazaki—Spoilers for *Princesss Mononoke* and *Nausicaä of the Valley of the Wind*
Review of Howl's Moving Castle—Spoiler free
Kon Capsules—Spoiler free
Four Kon Points—Spoilers for *Millennium Actress*
Millennium Actress Appendix—Spoilers for *Millennium Actress*
Godfathers: the Bright Side of Kon—Spoilers for *Tokyo Godfathers*
Kon Explores the Insanity of Japan—Spoilers for *Paranoia*

THE CHAMPION: HAYAO MIYAZAKI

MIYAZAKI WON
AN OSCAR

A Quick Guide to "Japan's Walt Disney"

It was an exciting moment for everyone when Hayao Miyazaki's *Spirited Away* (2001) won the Academy Award for Best Animated Feature at the 75th Academy Awards (2003): fans felt giddy that the anime boom had made such an award possible, while the newcomers found a wonderful new auteur to explore. It seemed as significant as the Oscar for Best Foreign Film in 1951 being awarded to Akira Kurosawa's *Rashomon*.

In the USA, Miyazaki was promoted as "Japan's Walt Disney," and this makes sense with a pair of his earlier films that have appropriate child-friendly movie ratings. But there is another side to Miyazaki, perhaps more like Kurosawa, with terrifying landscapes of warfare and destruction. Something more along the lines of *The Seven Samurai* or the Oscar-nominated *Ran*.

The Miyazaki Movies (and one music video) that will be mentioned in this study:

Nausicaä of the Valley of the Wind (1984)
Miyazaki's first feature is a post-apocalyptic epic. In a world destroyed by technological warfare, Nausicaä is a warrior princess of rifle and sword, an empathetic leader who is trying to save her kingdom from its neighbors, while striving to heal the world of its

ancient, man-made curse. 1h 57m, rated PG.

Castle in the Sky (1986)
An adventure movie set in a European type of place in a future post-technological time of steam power and dirigibles. An orphaned girl is being pursued by a sinister man and his men-in-derbies henchmen for the magical jewel she possesses; she befriends an orphaned boy who dreams of discovering the fabled castle in the sky, Laputa. 2h 6m, rated PG.

My Neighbor Totoro (1988)
Everybody loves "Totoro," even Akira Kurosawa, who ranked it among the top 100 films in the world!

This is the movie about magical childhood, where nooks and crannies have strange little creatures in them and friendly forest spirits move around, invisible to adults. Set in Japan circa 1955, a family of four has moved to the countryside to help the health of the ailing mother. The scholarly father works at home and the two daughters explore a natural world that becomes increasingly magical. 1h 28 m, rated G.

Kiki's Delivery Service (1989)
This is the coming-of-age story, where a young witch from the countryside struggles to earn a living in the big city, far from home. Set in the 1950s of an alternate history Europe in which there was no World War Two. 1h 43m, rated G.

Porco Rosso (1992)
This is an alternate history aircraft fantasy. Set in the 1920s in Italy, where air pirates take hostages for ransom, and a mysterious pig-faced man hunts them down. 1h 42m, rated PG.

"On Your Mark" (1995)
A soft-rock music video. In a futuristic metropolis, a militant cult has imprisoned a winged young woman. A violent SWAT police raid frees the prisoner, and two young officers try to help her learn

to fly.

Princess Mononoke (1997)
This is the dark movie, set in Japan at some point during the Muromachi period (AD 1336 to 1573). A stone-age prince, cursed by a demon and exiled from his village, goes forth into the world to discover why these terrible changes are happening. He finds a land of feuding samurai, but the real struggle is between two women: a technophilic Lady Eboshi who is rapacious of the land and insensitive to the gods, and the feral girl called "Mononoke," raised by a wolf goddess into a young woman who is anti-technology and anti-human. Pretty dark and violent for kids. 2h 14m, rated PG-13.

Spirited Away (2002)
The Oscar winner has a contemporary Japanese girl trapped in a weird Wonderland/fairy world, where she must work hard in order to save her ensorcelled parents so that the family can escape. The contemporary setting is surprising for Miyazaki, since his work is usually set in the future or the past. A little spooky for kids. 2h 5m, rated PG.

Howl's Moving Castle (2004)
In a steampunk world, a young woman is cursed into old age. She sets out to meet the infamous wizard Howl in the hope that he can help her, at a time when the world seems swinging inexorably toward war. 1h 59m, rated PG.

The Wind Rises (2021)
Miyazaki's final feature. A boy who dreams of designing planes grows up and invents the most famous Japanese aircraft of all. 2h 6m, rated PG-13.

FOUR MIYAZAKI POINTS

"Castle in the Sky" as Key to the Work of Miyazaki

(2005)

[Reconstructed from a video presentation given to an undergraduate class at Indiana University. They had watched Miyazaki's *Castle in the Sky* and I was using that as a springboard to talk about recurring elements in Miyazaki's work.]

Castle in the Sky (1986) is an excellent introduction to the works of Hayao Miyazaki as it shows four points Miyazaki returns to again and again in his movies: "Flight," "Technology versus Magic," "The Miyazaki Heroine," and "The Miyazaki Tree." This piece will compare and contrast *Castle in the Sky* with a number of other Miyazaki works, including the movies *Nausicaä of the Valley of the Wind* (1984), *My Neighbor Totoro* (1988), *Kiki's Delivery Service* (1989), *Porco Rosso* (1992), *Princess Mononoke* (1997), and the music video "On Your Mark" (1995).

These seven pieces by Miyazaki are all of the adventure type, in that the characters come out the same as they went in: for *Nausicaä of the Valley of the Wind, Castle in the Sky, My Neighbor*

Totoro, and "On Your Mark," the problem is solved, and things are back to normal; for *Kiki's Delivery Service, Porco Rosso,* and *Princess Mononoke,* the curse is lifted from the hero, who is back to normal.

·

Flight

Miyazaki has an enduring fascination with flight of all kinds. In *Castle in the Sky* his approach for powered flight is a steampunkish semi-realism. The airships are fairly realistic and plausible, only being a tad baroque and gigantic at times, whereas the flying platforms of the pirates are sci-fi whimsies.

Scene (0:00:49): Looking up below the pirate airship as the strange flying platforms are launched, each like a horseless chariot with dragonfly wings.

Scene (0:01:31): The lumbering superlarge airship, the target of the pirates. With graceful maneuverings, the pirates prepare to storm the bridge.

In the post-apocalyptic *Nausicaä,* Miyazaki uses a similar approach but trades the Victorian airships for WWII aircraft. Again the vehicles are extra massive, but where this supersizing makes the airships seem baroque, it makes the bombers seem more crude and brutal.

Scene (0:28:49): A flying armada of weird superheavy bombers, some having an "H" shape with wings in fore and aft.

Scene (0:46:30): A single fighter plane swoops down, guns blazing. A bomber catches fire, dips down, explodes. The bombers return fire, but the fighter climbs up again and destroys another.

Miyazaki is not limited to technological flight—in fact, he seems very eager for magical flight as well, as evidenced in *My Neighbor Totoro.*

> *Scene (0:59:32): A wooden top is spinning on the ground. The two smaller Totoros jump onto the chest of Totoro, and little girl Mei does the same. Totoro hops onto the top. Mei's big sister Satsuki leaps onto Totoro's chest, and then they all ride the top up into the air, soaring higher than the trees, where they roar with delight.*

Both technological flight and magical flight are in *Kiki's Delivery Service,* where the young witch is already flying in the opening credits.

> *Scene (opening credits 0:08:34): Thirteen-year-old Kiki rides her flying broom through the night sky over a highway dotted with the headlights of driving cars. A large passenger plane with stacked wings and a box-kite tail section passes by her, well overhead.*

> *Scene (1:18:46): A zeppelin-like airship flies by the bakery. The baker waves enthusiastically.*

Porco Rosso seems like Miyazaki's love letter to realistic airplanes. Most of the planes look very realistic, drawn straight from history, and even though the planes of the air pirates are again large, crude, and deadly, they are not so over-the-top as the bombers in *Nausicaä.*

> *Scene (0:05:01): Porco Rosso, the flying bounty hunter, spots a passenger plane and peels over to investigate. It is a sightseeing flight filled with young women. He warns them to be wary.*

Scene (0:06:15): The air pirates have captured a full cargo of vacationing schoolgirls, but before they can get to their base, Porco Rosso pounces upon them. Porco deftly shoots out their engines, clips their wings, and forces them to make splash-landings in the Adriatic.

The music video "On Your Mark" is different for being Miyazaki's only foray into cyberpunk territory. This is highly unusual, since his preferred technology is either old fashioned or weird futured, rather than the cold sterility of science fiction, yet even so, he presents flight.

Scene (0:34): Police jet-powered troop landers zoom across a cyberpunk cityscape toward a tower with a neon eye. Purposefully they crash into the tower and disgorge shock troops. A firefight ensues between police and militant cultists.

Scene (3:51): A police aircar tries to halt a fleeing ground car on a narrow skybridge. The hero refuses to stop the car, pressing ahead. The ground car hits the aircar, the aircar explodes, the bridge breaks up, and the car begins to fall.

.

Technology versus Magic

Miyazaki often sets up worlds where technology and magic are both valid systems. In *Castle in the Sky*, the "magic" is really a highly advanced technology, yet it remains mysteriously magical. In the case of flight, we have Pazu's long labor at building a plane, in contrast to Sheeta's magical necklace.

Scene (0:15:44): In the boy Pazu's workshop, the girl Sheeta sees his work in progress, a flying machine with bird-like wings, looking like something based on a drawing by Leonardo da Vinci.

Scene (0:26:29): Dangling over an abyss, Pazu clutches Sheeta with one arm and holds to a broken bridge with his free hand. The bridge finally gives way and the two children fall into the yawning canyon, but halfway down Sheeta's necklace begins to glow and they find themselves magically floating down.

In *Nausicaä*, again the magic is really a high technology, as seen in the contrast between two aircraft: a "brig" and a flying wing "mehve."

Scene (1:18:42): Nausicaä and Asbel see a "brig" land. To our eyes it is a strange design, but it is clearly an airplane.

Scene (opening credits 0:03:20): Nausicaä's signature vehicle, the "mehve," is so advanced in its design that it is more magical than technological. The near-equivalent of a flying broom.

Then again, for *Kiki* it really is technology and magic. As in *Castle in the Sky,* the boy is working on a plane, and the girl can already fly magically.

Scene (1:07:08): The boy-inventor Tombo shows Kiki his work in progress—a big propeller mounted on the front of a bicycle, as a precursor to a man-powered airplane. He offers to take her on a street ride to the beach, and she accepts but admits that she has never been on a bike before.

Scene (0:21:03): Kiki offers to help the baker's wife by delivering to a distant customer an item left behind at the shop. The heavily pregnant wife assumes the girl will run and is impressed when Kiki mounts her broom and launches off the cliff to fly sedately toward the customer.

"On Your Mark" also keeps the hard line between technology and magic, in this case with the brutal police aircraft contrasting with the gentle angel.

Scene (0:34): Police troop landers fly over the cyberpunk cityscape [again].

Scene (1:27): Inside the tower of the cultists, the heroes discover an angel-like being held as a chained captive. She has big white feathery wings. Dissolve to the trio in an open-top sports car, where the heroes are training the angel to spread her wings and fly.

.

The Miyazaki Heroine

The Miyazaki Heroine has short hair, sports a slim figure, and is either something of a tomboy or an outright warrior.

Sheeta of *Castle in the Sky* is a princess with enough moxie to be a co-star rather than a simple quest object. The struggle of her heart is over the mystery of her legacy, tied up with the anti-gravity nodes. While she has long hair for most of the film, this abruptly changes near the end.

Scene (1:53:08): The villain shoots at Sheeta, proving his marksmanship by cutting off one of her braids, and then the other.

Scene (1:59:12): Sheeta and Pazu in a glider escape the rising ruins of Laputa. Now her hair is short.

Nausicaä is a warrior princess. She is skilled at fighting, and the struggle of her heart is regarding the use of force. She also has a tenderness for animals.

Scene (0:13:59): Nausicaä plays with the cute animal and asks Master Yuppa if she can keep it.

Satsuki in *Totoro* is a young girl, but she is also a big sister. She struggles with fears over her mother's illness, and later over the disappearance of her sister.

Scene (1:12:50): Satsuki runs across the countryside, searching and calling for her missing sister Mei.

Kiki is a teen going out on a required year away from home to prove herself as a competent witch. Her slogan is about the pureness of her heart.

Scene (0:00:24): Kiki lies in the grass, listening to the weather report, then rises up and hurries home, ready to embark on her adventure.

Mononoke is the opposite of Nausicaä, being a feral warrior princess. Her struggle is to let go of her own anti-humanism, which is somewhat similar to how Sheeta must reject her own evil legacy in *Castle in the Sky*.

Scene (0:22:22): Mononoke performs first aid on a wounded wolf god by sucking blood from a bullet hole and spitting it out.

.

The Miyazaki Tree
Miyazaki often has an unusual tree prominently placed in his work. This tree is always a guardian, a protector, a sentinel. Often it purifies or heals.

The tree in *Castle in the Sky* is the one massive tree that has outgrown the botanical garden, to the point that it dominates the entire cloud city—it represents Life in the ruins. When the city breaks apart at the end, it is revealed that the tree's roots reach all the way to the anti-gravity nodes.

> *Scene (1:31:16): Sheeta and Pazu discover the giant tree that has overgrown the cloud city.*

> *Scene (1:57:21): After most of the city has fallen away, the air pirates can see the nodes of anti-gravity, now entangled in the roots of the tree.*

> *Scene (end credits): The ruins of the cloud city Laputa are in orbit, where the tree is a guardian against humans once again obtaining the dangerous nodes of anti-gravity.*

In *Nausicaä*, the heroine regains consciousness in a weird crystalline forest/cave structure. Asbel tells her they are beneath the poisoned sands of the wasteland. She is surprised to learn that the air is clean, purified by the "trees."

> *Scene (1:03:50): Nausicaä wakes up in a mysterious place. Asbel tells her they are beneath the wasteland, and she is shocked to learn that the air has been detoxified by the towering crystal formations.*

In *Totoro*, the sisters Satsuki and Mei visit the giant camphor tree in their new neighborhood. It has a shrine at its base and a sacred rope around its trunk.

> *Scene (39:27): Stirring music as the children take in the amazing sight of the god-like tree.*

In *Princess Mononoke*, Mononoke takes the mortally wounded

Ashitaka across a mysterious lake to an island of life and death, where stands a large tree.

Scene (59:32): Across the lake to the island of life and death, and its lone tree.

.

These then are the four things so common to Miyazaki movies: Flight, Technology versus Magic, the Miyazaki Heroine, and the Miyazaki Tree. Through the course of his films, Miyazaki returns to these things, sometimes continuing a sequence (Pazu's unfinished plane and then Tombo's preparation for test flight), sometimes doing the same but with a difference (Nausicaä and Mononoke, despite being polar opposites in most ways, are both warriors who learn that violence is not always the answer).

KIKI'S TEXT INTO FILM

(2004)

Hayao Miyazaki usually works from original scripts, but one exception is *Kiki's Delivery Service* (1989), based on a novel by Eiko Kadono. In book and film, Kiki is a young witch who leaves home to work her craft in a distant city for one year. She sets out on this adventure with only her cat-familiar Jiji, her flying broom, and a transistor radio. She soon finds herself in a coastal city where her only marketable talent is her ability to fly, so she starts a one-witch flying delivery service. Supporting characters include Osano, wife of a baker (she gives Kiki a spare room to stay in), and Tombo, a neighborhood boy who is obsessed with flight.

One immediately wonders how Miyazaki reworks a text written by someone else, and to what degree he invents new plot lines and adds characters to create further conflict. For the short answer, Helen McCarthy provides an overview on Miyazaki and the original novel:

> *[Miyazaki] needed to transform it into a story that would support a feature-length film. The original novel is episodic and lighthearted. Kiki meets with no terrible challenges or traumas, she has no crisis of self-belief like the one in the movie, and the dramatic end sequence with the airship is missing altogether. In a movie for young people, the hero*

*needs to grow through vivid, dramatic struggle and lone-
liness. (Hayao Miyazaki: Master of Japanese Animation,
142)*

For the medium answer, the movie is made of chapters 1 through 6; chapters 7 through 11 are largely ignored. Miyazaki compressed the first two chapters into the pre-opening credits section of the movie. He then followed chapters 3 and 4 fairly closely but incorporated elements from later chapters. Material from chapters 5 and 6 were rearranged and reworked into the remainder of the movie, with some elements drawn from later chapters. This made the plotline more dramatic and focused.

For the long answer, I will first outline the novel, and then compare the movie to the book.

Kadono's *Kiki's Delivery Service*

Kadono's novel for young readers (age nine and up) has eleven chapters:

1. "Bells in the Treetops": Kiki's mother urges her to go off on her year away from home, but Kiki resists.
2. "A New Witch's Broom": Kiki checks on her secret project, a new flying broom, and decides to start her trip soon after all.
3. "Kiki in the Big City": Kiki finally sets out, travels, and arrives.
4. "Kiki Open for Business": the baker's wife Osano has her baby; Kiki's first job (delivery of a bird cage and cat toy as birthday present); Kiki meets an artist.
5. "The Broom Thief": Kiki goes to the beach, where a sudden storm draws her cat Jiji and a boy out to sea; Kiki rides a bucking false broom, substituted by a thief, and manages to rescue cat and boy; Tombo, the boy who stole the broom, tries to fly it, but he crashes and the broom breaks.
6. "Kiki in the Doldrums": the artist's portrait of Kiki is done (Kiki's job is to deliver it somewhere); Violet the washerwoman uses Kiki as a flying clothesline.

7. "Kiki Shares a Secret": the girl in pink (Mimi) hires Kiki to deliver an anonymous letter and present to a boy; Kiki peeks at the letter, loses the letter, rewrites the poem from memory on a leaf, and delivers it. It all works out anyway and Mimi becomes friends with Kiki.

8. "Kiki to the Captain's Rescue": a granny hires Kiki to deliver a belly wrap to the steam tug; at the steam tug they are trying to deliver rare wine and need some help.

9. "Kiki Rings in the New Year": there is trouble at the clock tower. Kiki is told by town authorities to steal a clock gear from a neighboring town, but she cannot, so she flies fast and moves the clock hand by herself.

10. "Kiki Carries the Sounds of Spring": a classical music group arrives in town to give a concert but their instruments are mistakenly left on the train. Kiki must chase and board the moving train; then she brings the instruments to the concert, with the wind of her passage making music all the way.

11. "Kiki Goes Home": at the end of her year away, Kiki goes home for a visit but realizes she misses the city and can't wait to get back.

Comparing Movie to Book

A. The movie's beginning is much tighter. The book has mother Kokiri urging Kiki, with Kiki resisting. Then Kiki decides, checks her new broom, announces to parents—now Kokiri is surprised and resisting. The movie opens with Kiki lying on a grassy hill, a detail of her habits revealed much later in the book (Chapter 5), then hits the highlights (including the scene where Kiki's father holds her up to "fly" one more time, a part I would have bet was a Miyazaki invention) and goes, two chapters compressed into 8 minutes before the opening credits roll.

B. The movie's rain, train, and encounter with cows on the flight to the city is a Miyazaki creation since there is nothing like this in book, but the harrowing train chase in Chapter 10 seems related to Kiki's flying departure from the moving train in the film. (The unexpected travel by train also echoes the spirit train of *Grave of the Fireflies* [1988], another Ghibli film, and anticipates the ghost train in Miyazaki's *Spirited Away*.)

C. Kiki's arrival at the city, traffic trouble, a cry of "thief!" The arrival is fairly close to the book, but Miyazaki invents both the traffic trouble caused by her flying and the subsequent arrival of the police officer who investigates the near accidents. The false cry of "thief" by Tombo (a ploy to allow Kiki to escape from the officer) is an interesting twist on Chapter 5 where Tombo is the thief of Kiki's broom.

D. Kiki's first job. There are some minor differences: in the book Kiki gets her own phone (in the movie she uses the bakery's phone); Kiki drops the cat toy through Jiji's mischief and simply cannot find it in time (in the movie Kiki has to deal with angry crows); to rescue Jiji from his role as a toy cat, Kiki just goes in through a window (the movie invents Jeff the dog both to drive up tension of Jiji's discovery and to provide rescue for Jiji).

There is a major difference in the fact that the artist who finds the cat toy is not named in the book, but Ursula the artist is a pivotal character in the movie.

Kiki's first job is slightly boosted into the movie's first crisis. Kiki learns that things can go wrong, but if she just puts in the extra effort and does the right things, it will all work out in the end.

E. Invitation to a party. While the book has Tombo in a flying club, Miyazaki invents the party Tombo invites Kiki to. This heightens tension as Kiki's job for Madame leads to a schedule conflict with the party.

F. Madame, Bertha, and Madame's granddaughter the girl in pink. Here Miyazaki creates characters and situations, increasing the tension to the movie's second crisis: Kiki's extra effort (she helps

Madame bake the birthday pie) and her trip through a downpour to deliver the pie are met with disdain by Madame's granddaughter, the girl in pink (she does not want the pie). Crushed by this result, Kiki misses the party with Tombo.

The movie's Madame (who wants to bake a pie for her granddaughter's birthday) is somewhat similar to the knitting granny of Chapter 8 (who wants Kiki to deliver the product of her own hands to a relative) and Violet of Chapter 6 (who wants Kiki to deliver biscuits to her sister across town); Bertha, Madame's servant, is like Violet as washerwoman; the girl in pink is very much like Mimi of Chapter 7 but harsher and with no "becoming friends" with Kiki later. Miyazaki has taken characters from the text, altered them, and then interlinked them.

G. Kiki getting sick, recovering, taking package to Tombo, riding flying bicycle—not in the book. Miyazaki accelerates the relationship between Kiki and Tombo—their ride on the bicycle is the third crisis of the movie, which resolves with a magical flight and laughter of relief, yet the good feelings are brought short by the arrival of the girl in pink, clearly Kiki's nemesis at this point.

The relationship between Kiki and Tombo is slower in the book. The movie perhaps infuses the romance of Chapter 7 (Mimi's love letter and gift to a boy) into Tombo's courtship of Kiki, and Kiki's growing awareness of the pampered "pretty girls" around her going on dates and attending parties, in contrast to independent (and lonely) "working girl" Kiki.

The crash of the flying bike is an interesting twist on Chapter 5 where Tombo crashes the stolen broom and breaks it. While there is no flying bike in the book, the club is researching flight (one team investigating flying shoes, one team looking into flying carpets, and a third team examining witches' brooms); furthermore, Tombo invents a helium balloon tether so that Kiki can carry unusual objects (the portrait in Chapter 6). So maybe book-Tombo's inventiveness, interest in flight, and use of lighter-than-air gases leads to not only the movie's bike plane (Tombo's invention) but also the movie's zeppelin.

H. Kiki's doldrums, the movie's fourth crisis, is thus much more intense than Chapter 6 of the book: after the flight of the bike she has lost her magic; she is the one who breaks the broom while trying to fly off a steep hill (the book has Tombo do exactly this in Chapter 5). Ursula comes to rescue Kiki, inviting the young witch to her cabin for recuperation (the book has the nameless artist call Kiki to pick up and deliver the portrait of Kiki and Jiji, that's all).

I. The movie's final climax is another Miyazaki invention. Returning to the city from the cabin, Kiki gets a telephone message from Osano to visit Madame. It turns out that Madame has a birthday-style cake for Kiki, so when Kiki receives this gift in teary delight the terrible wound caused by the girl in pink (the rejection of the birthday pie) is healed. This closes the loop of the second crisis.

The happiness is interrupted by disaster on the live TV broadcast of the zeppelin landing that Bertha is watching: a sudden wind makes the airship buck and all the rope-holding ground-crew are shaken off except for Kiki's friend Tombo, who clings to the nose line as the airship takes off to drift across town. Kiki cannot fly anymore, so she races on foot through the city streets. The zeppelin hits the clocktower and stays there, but Tombo is still stranded. Frantic, Kiki borrows a pushbroom from a street sweeper. Miraculously she is able to fly with it (resolving the fourth crisis), but it bucks, twists, and drops on her (validating the warnings of her mother at the beginning about riding "raw" brooms): the resulting hair-raising flight returns to the traffic trouble Kiki caused on her first arrival to the city. Kiki makes a few attempts to close with Tombo, but finally his grip slips and he falls, at which instant Kiki goes into a powered dive and grabs his hand (echoing the powered dive that failed to catch the birdcage in her first job: thus closing the loop on the first crisis). They land safely to the cheers of the townspeople, and Kiki is her old self again. (Across town, a relieved Osano goes into labor after seeing the rescue on TV. This birthing, which is just an aside in Chapter 4, takes on much more symbolic meaning.)

The movie's climax is a blend of the book's rescue in Chapter 5 (a sudden storm, the quest to save a friend from death while using a normal broom that bucks) and the hard work of fixing the clock tower (while the whole town is watching) in Chapter 9. There are also trace elements of Chapter 8 (the steamboat captain needing help is now an airship captain).

J. The notion of city girls adopting the "witch look" *a la* Kiki comes up early in book (Chapter 5) but only at end of the movie (in images during closing credits).

So, in focusing the movie on chapters 1 through 6 and rearranging or inventing events, Miyazaki heightens the tension and the throughline of the film version.

·

More from the Book: the Look and the Technology
The original book was illustrated, and Miyazaki seems to have followed the look quite closely. The town layout and style matches that found in the book. The only difference is Kiki's hair being shorter in the movie.

The book is very vague as to the technological level of the world: Kiki has a transistor radio, Tombo has a bike, and there are trains, but the one boat we see is a steamboat. Are there any cars? More importantly, are there any planes? That is, what does "human flight" mean to these people? The investigations of Tombo's club (flying shoes, flying carpets, flying brooms) might be either mundane/childish or alternate Earth/practical, depending on the answer.

Miyazaki solves this by setting the movie in an alternate 1950s where there was no World War Two, so there are still old style cars, airplanes, and even airships.

·

I have a new appreciation for how Miyazaki took an episodic novel and turned it into a feature film. I think the choices he made were excellent and I feel that he managed to capture the spirit of the work even those cases where he was "making it up" (for example, the climactic rescue of Tombo from the zeppelin is an amplified version of the book's rescue of Jiji from the sea tide). He built up Tombo from a sneak into the boy who loved Kiki at first sight and the friend who had to be rescued; he expanded the nameless artist into Ursula, the elder version of Kiki, role-model and big sister; he turned Mimi into the anonymous girl in pink, a class-snob "party girl" rival for Tombo's attention, whose callous rejection of the pie baked by her grandmother triggers Kiki's doldrums; he added period aircraft to show the difference between mundane human flight and magical witch flight, the distinctions of which are then blurred in the breathtaking first-flight of the bicycle-plane.

Books

Kadono, Eiko. *Kiki's Delivery Service.* Toronto: Annick Press, 2003.

McCarthy, Helen. *Hayao Miyazaki: Master of Japanese Animation.* Berkeley: Stone Bridge Press, 1999.

KIKI'S ITALIAN MODEL

(2021)

It is clear that Hayao Miyazaki has a deep affinity for things Italian. "Ghibli," the name of his studio, "is a word for a strong Saharan wind and also the name of one of Miyazaki's favorite Italian airplanes" (McCarthy, 42). That airplane is the Caproni Ca.309, from the Caproni company founded by Giovanni Battista Caproni. Caproni's planes increasingly haunt Miyazaki's skies, and Caproni's name first shows up in semi-disguise with Tombo Kopoli, the flying bike engineer in *Kiki's Delivery Service.*

Even with all this evidence, it is a staggering surprise that Miyazaki secretly made homage to an obscure Italian art house film: compare the opening of Miyazaki's *Kiki's Delivery Service* (1989) to that of Antonio Pietrangeli's *I Knew Her Well* (1965).

Kiki's Delivery Service (first 2 minutes)

A radio announcer is talking about news and weather. The location is a grassy hillside overlooking water. Tracking right to show the girl KIKI lying in the grass, the big red bow in her hair flopping in the breeze.

Cut to show Kiki in profile, looking up at the sky. Shots of beautiful nature, in clouds above and a bee buzzing by.

Hearing some detail in the news, Kiki makes a decision. She turns off her radio, gets up, walks.

Moving faster, she passes around a hedge and hops over a puddle.

She runs down a dirt road, a man on bicycle going the other way.

She runs into the yard of her home and inside to her mother's lab, where her mother is mixing a magic potion for a customer. Kiki announces she will leave that night.

I Knew Her Well (first 3 minutes)

Instrumental pop music is playing as scene opens on a beach without people, pivoting left, from folded umbrellas across sand to water. Credits roll. The beach is not swept or clean: there are bits of trash, presumably from previous visitors. Across the shoreline, then to sand again. The broken ruins of a rowboat. Pan down to bare feet in the sand, soles up. Pan up along her bare legs to reveal ADRIANA, a young woman napping belly down on a beach blanket. The song ends and an announcer speaks, revealing that the pop music has been playing on the woman's transistor radio.

The radio announcer gives the time, and the woman abruptly rises, gathers up her material, and hurries off.

Running along on the city street in her clattering wooden sandals, she stops to have an ice seller fasten the back of her bikini top, then scampers on her clattering way.

Cut to street scene where a man is hosing down the sidewalk. Adriana asks him for a quick spray of water.

At last, she arrives at the beauty shop where she works. She takes a quick nap, then cut to scene where she is working on a customer.

•

It is remarkable to recognize such a clear homage as Miyazaki makes to the obscure Italian film. Miyazaki copies the pattern of music, the landscape, the reclining heroine; her radio, her hurry; the shop, the customer.

Miyazaki was clearly on to something, since Pietrangeli's *I Knew Her Well* bears similarities to Kadono's novel *Kiki's Delivery*

Service. Both feature young women from the countryside struggling to make a living in the city; both works are made up of vignettes that alternate between comedy, slice of life, and drama. But *Kiki's Delivery Service* is a light-hearted adventure novel for pre-teens, while *I Knew Her Well* is a dark, cautionary tale for young women.

Miyazaki obviously modeled his movie's opening off of the opening to *I Knew Her Well,* but he also drew something from the ending of Pietrangeli's movie.

In discussing the text to film translation in the prior chapter, I noted that the climax of the movie is a blend of storm/rescue, bucking brooms, and clocktower repair in the book. While this is true, important elements are added by *I Knew Her Well.*

The body of Pietrangeli's film is a series of vignettes, each one more degrading to the heroine Adriana than the last. Then she hits rock bottom and begins to rise up, having a wild night of exciting sensations and settling old scores.

The morning after finds Adriana listening to records in her upper story apartment. She puts on her favorite song, a "Bunny Hop" tune, and arranges things on her desk. She looks out the window at the city. She takes off her wig. As the song ends, we see the clouds, as if through her eyes, and then a blur of falling outside to smash into the ground below. Adriana has jumped to her death.

Miyazaki has taken this suicidal tragedy and crafted a heroic happy ending by having an angel catch a falling loved one, saving him from death.

It is clear that Miyazaki's version of Kiki has a secret inspiration in Pietrangeli's *I Knew Her Well.* (This is a lot bigger than the one-off moment in Miyazaki's *Castle in the Sky* [1986] where the invaders are looting the city, a scene that comes straight from the Soviet movie version of *War and Peace* [1966/67], where Napoleon's soldiers are despoiling Moscow.) What seems initially a framing device, copying the beginning and bending the ending of the Italian film, in reality points to deeper layers of sympathy.

MONONOKE: THE DARK SIDE OF MIYAZAKI

(2021)

Princess Mononoke (1997), Miyazaki's sixth film for Studio Ghibli, is his darkest film. A sort of "Twilight of the Gods," it is set in 16th century Japan, a time when feudalism had broken down, giving rise to the Warring States period. But Miyazaki had originally envisioned something more like the fairy tale "Beauty and the Beast." As Helen McCarthy puts it in *Hayao Miyazaki: Master of Japanese Animation,*

> *Miyazaki had made sketches in the late seventies for a movie about a beautiful princess living in the woods with a savage beast . . . a* mononoke, *a beast-spirit who strongly resembled the Catbus in* My Neighbor Totoro *. . . The project was turned down . . . Miyazaki returned to the idea almost fifteen years later. (McCarthy, 182)*

To be clear, the Catbus for *My Neighbor Totoro* (1988) turns out to have been recycled from the beastly bridegroom of Miyazaki's rejected "Beauty and the Beast" proposal in the 1970s. Furthermore, despite this early setback, Miyazaki successfully used "Beauty and the Beast" as a main driver for *Porco Rosso* (1992).

It seems that when Miyazaki picked up the "mononoke" concept again, he radically shifted things by fleshing it out with a reworking of characters and conflict from his own *Nausicaä of the Valley of the Wind* (1984). The role of "peace warrior" pioneered by Princess Nausicaä was assigned to stone-age Ashitaka; the character of obsessed, one-armed leader Kushana became Iron Town's Lady Eboshi; the "prince without a kingdom" Asbel was added to Ashitaka as the cursed exile. The great beings who must be propitiated, the Ohmu, who had killed and resurrected Nausicaä at the end of her movie, were invested into the giant forest god. The character of feral girl Mononoke (hereafter referred to by her wolf name "San") is missing from this lineup, but I suspect she is a translation of Teto, the wild squirrel fox that Nausicaä tames into a pet through her own blood, suffering, and gentle nature. The revamped story gives a stark battle between two sides: San wants to kill all humans, and Lady Eboshi wants to kill all gods. Ashitaka tries to mediate, but Lady Eboshi manages to decapitate the forest god before having her arm bitten off by a dying wolf god. Clearly, this is a long way from "Beauty and the Beast."

When Miyazaki moves the *Nausicaä* scenario from the science fiction future into the fantasy past, the gods become real gods, and the brewing conflict more directly resembles Norse myth's Ragnarök, a word translated as "Fate of the Gods" or "Twilight of the Gods." The main event of Ragnarök is an apocalyptic battle between gods and monsters, a fight in which many gods die: the god Odin is swallowed by the monster wolf Fenrir, and the god Thor is killed by the world serpent. (A strong parallel to Miyazaki's one-armed character Kushana is the Norse god Tyr, who had previously lost his arm to the monster wolf Fenrir, and at the final battle Tyr is killed by the monster dog Garm. This detail linking Kushana to Tyr suggests Miyazaki drew inspiration from Ragnarök for *Nausicaä*.) Most of the Norse monsters are killed as well, but the unvanquished giant Sutr spreads flames that destroy the world. Then the world is rebuilt, and two new humans are formed to populate it.

However, despite the strong evidence that Miyazaki draws

deeply from "Beauty and the Beast," *Nausicaä,* and Ragnarök, he nevertheless dodges all three implied endings. Riding the tension for all it is worth, he nixes the fairytale ending of marriage in "Beauty and the Beast"; he eschews the Hollywood ending of messianic validation in *Nausicaä;* and he shies away from total world reset of Ragnarök. Despite all appearances, the climax of *Princess Mononoke* is not the destruction of the world or the end of an age, it is just a Wednesday. Notice that Miyazaki passes over the cleanbreak ending of *Casablanca* ("We'll always have Iron Town, San"). Basically, Miyazaki opts for the "no commitment" ending of *Kiki's Delivery Service* (1989) rather than the marriage ending of *Porco Rosso.*

Princess Mononoke is not the clone of *Nausicaä of the Valley of the Wind:* it is the evil twin. The forest god is the only "good guy" in the film. He has two forms: during the day he is the crowned stag, and at sunset he grows into the giant reptilian Night Walker (Daidarabotchi). Since San is an agent of the forest god, and San's attitude is "kill all humans," it suggests that the forest god is accepting of a "kill all humans" agenda.

Miyazaki is bold in sharpening the conflict from *Nausicaä* into a Nietzschean "Humanity against the Gods" deal, and making the opposing champions sympathetic females. There is a certain amount of whitewashing for both sides: the gods do not require regular human sacrifice, and Iron Town is compassionately supportive of lepers. (The scene of women doing factory work also reflects Miyazaki's personal family history and the experience of World War Two, where Japanese women worked in the factories churning out weapons. Miyazaki's family owned a factory that made parts for the Japanese Zero. The image of women working at such heavy industry also shows up in Miyazaki's film *Porco Rosso,* where Italian women are building the hero's airplane.) But both San and Lady Eboshi are obviously broken: the young orphan is so alienated from her roots that she hates all humans; and Lady Eboshi is so drunk on power she wants to kill a god of nature. Miyazaki is daring for driving the viewers to root for the gods, to side with the losing side: since this film is set in the past, the viewer knows that the gods have diminished further in the zero-sum fashion just as technology has grown. Siding with the losing side in fiction has a long history, since the ancient Greeks did it with their former foes the Trojans, and then later with the Persians; more recent cases are Dixie, and of course Imperial Japan, but these examples have the dangerous tang to them, the romance of the Noble Lost Cause. Miyazaki wisely guards against this by presenting both champions and their respective factions as broken.

Miyazaki depicts gods who exhibit two traits associated with fairies rather than gods: a shrinking in size, and a pronounced aversion to iron. For the first, McCarthy notes about the movie, "[the] beast gods see their children growing up smaller than they themselves are, literally diminishing in stature as their powers diminish" (McCarthy, 193). This trait does not derive from Norse mythology; instead it comes straight from theories about the origin of fairies: "A . . . theory holds that fairies are discarded gods . . . reduced in stature and importance as an old set of gods gives way to a new" (*Funk & Wagnalls Standard Dictionary of Folklore, Mythology, and Legend*, "fairy" entry). The hatred of the movie's gods for iron is less direct: the gods are especially vulnerable to firearms, weapons that are a product of Lady Eboshi's Iron Town. The entry on "iron" in *Funk & Wagnalls* begins: "This metal enters into the folklore of most peoples either in religious tabus or as a charm against supernaturals and sorcery." Later, it states, "The power of iron to drive off and keep out evil spirits and supernatural beings of all kinds is almost universal."

In summary, the motion picture *Princess Mononoke* has roots in fairy tale's "Beauty and the Beast," Miyazaki's *Nausicaä of the Valley of the Wind,* and the Norse Ragnarök. While Miyazaki obscures much of the "Beauty and the Beast" story, including the ending, still fairy tale elements pop up again in the movie's gods having traits associated with fairies. The film's convention-defying conclusion has the effect of de-emphasizing the two young heroes, treating them as mere pawns of their respective factions. Because the movie is an adventure type, the characters emerge only slightly changed: humans remain a curse on the planet.

Books

Leach, Maria and Jerome Fried. *Funk & Wagnalls Standard Dictionary of Folklore, Mythology, and Legend.* New York: Harper & Row, 1984.

McCarthy, Helen. *Hayao Miyazaki: Master of Japanese Animation.* Berkeley: Stone Bridge Press, 1999.

REVIEW OF HOWL'S MOVING CASTLE

*(2005: The Internet Review
of Science Fiction)*

Howl's Moving Castle (2004), the latest animated movie by Hayao Miyazaki, is an excellent introduction for mainstream Americans to the work of this Academy Award–winning director, but fans of the book will likely be disappointed unless they check their expectations at the door.

The story is about a young woman named Sophie who is cursed by a witch so that her body becomes that of a 90-year-old woman. After fleeing her mother's house to avoid being seen by her family, Sophie sets out to catch the mobile residence of the wizard Howl, a flamboyant despoiler of young women. As a sudden-crone she feels safe from his alleged appetites, so she installs herself as castle-cleaner in the hope of finding a way to break the curse, with or without Howl's help.

The movie is a visual delight, conjured forth in the beautiful hand-drawn style for which Miyazaki is famous. The beginning is airy and light, a wedding cake for the eyes, revealing a steam age setting where the air is crowded with cigar-shaped ornithopters bearing messengers and pleasure-seekers, while gallant soldiers court pretty maids and a steam-powered car chuffs down the cobblestone street below. But the European-styled kingdoms, true to their 19th century form, bluster their way toward warfare. And the war, when it comes, is savage, frightening, and point-less, bringing darkness. At one memorable point, techno-magical heavy bombers escorted by strange flying demons drop loads of bombs onto the cute and charming city, where the cobblestone streets erupt in flames and flying shrapnel.

The mixture of steam technology and magic gives the movie a steampunk feel, as does the introduction of World War Two–style aerial bombardment into such a bright and tidy land. These elements (steam and magic; flight, technological and magical; anti-war sentiments) are all close to Miyazaki's heart, showing up in his seven other movies at Studio Ghibli. Not the least, in So-phie we find another form of the Miyazaki heroine, a plucky girl who rises to the challenges presented by outrageous misfortune in each of his films.

With regard to the central characters, the movie is true to the book or even improves upon it. The character of Sophie is most faithful to the text. The witch's curse shakes Sophie from her too-timid existence: even as she is burdened by the aches and pains of old age, she is also emboldened to speak out with the assumed conviction of elderly wisdom, to act as a grandmother when she is not yet a mother. Playing the role of an old woman frees her from the role of being a dutiful daughter, allowing her to bloom in un-expected ways.

Howl, the heart-stealing wizard, is adequately translated from the text. Depicted as flashy and semi-androgynous in the way of a rock star like David Bowie, his extroverted, colorful na-ture makes him the opposite of pre-cursed Sophie. Yet we learn that Howl is playing a number of different roles himself, as well as suffering a curse of his own.

The character of the moving castle itself has no analog in the novel—it is pure Miyazaki, a whimsical chimera of biological-seeming mechanical and architectural elements: a drawbridge mouth, factory smokestacks like spines or plumes, turrets that look like eyes, and massive robotic chicken-legs, with which it walks around the countryside. This silent yet expressive character is a steampunk version of Baba Yaga's hut and validates the story's title more fully than the novel does.

But there are major differences between the movie and the book, mainly in the world of the setting and in the plot.

Diana Wynne Jones's book (of the same title, published in 1986) is not at all a steampunk novel. It is nearly the opposite: a realistic-seeming world that follows fairytale rules. For example, Sophie is the eldest of three sisters, and since in fairytales nothing good ever comes to the eldest, her culture sees her as doomed. Sophie agrees, and to avoid making matters worse for herself she lives a quiet, mousy life of hard work, low self-esteem, and lower expectations. That is to say, she was cursed by her birth-order long before the witch transformed her.

Rather than the wing-flapping flying machines, the novel features a more traditional fairytale artifact, the seven-league boots. Sophie must use these boots to quickly get from one place to another, yet she does not know exactly how to use them, which makes for a charming and exciting episode.

The novel's plot is convoluted in the way that fairytales often are, but it is not a satire or a parody; it is a rigorous playing-out of fairytale logic. Miyazaki's movie is not "about" fairytales in the way the book is, so Miyazaki's version is Sophie-centric, highly streamlined, and somewhat sketchy toward the edges.

Miyazaki's film is set in a solidly British steampunky fantasy world without the slightest trace of Japan about it. This may in fact be its greatest strength, since American audiences might have been put off by the Asian elements of Miyazaki's movies: the recent films *Princess Mononoke* (1997) and the Oscar Award-winning *Spirited Away* (2001) are set in Japan, which raises all sorts of cultural barriers for the uninitiated. These two Japanocentric films came out precisely at the moment when Disney was bringing Miyazaki movies to American theaters. In contrast, *Howl's Moving Castle* is readily accessible to the mainstream audience, yet at the same time it is not at all a generic fantasy: it is a work of originality and beauty that will win over viewers of all ages.

•

I have a certain amount of sympathy for Disney in distributing Miyazaki's work. At the time when they were hammering out their agreement, Miyazaki's recent films were "Totoro," "Kiki," and "Porco," which are all very kid-friendly movies (two of the three are also in a European setting). Once the agreement was in place, out came "Mononoke," Miyazaki's darkest and most violent movie. Disney could not exactly release this "Twilight of the Gods" picture under the Disney label, so they went the Miramax route. One might debate that the violence may have been more of a hurdle for American audiences, but that it is also set in medieval Japan is a further difficulty.

Only two of the eight movies to date are based upon the work of another. The majority (75%) were written by Miyazaki himself.

I happen to think that "Kiki" is a better adaptation, but then again, that book is very episodic and open-ended, which helps a lot. The main difference is that book-Kiki is a cool teen (as seen by a pre-teen readership), whereas movie-Kiki is a coming-of-age heroine depicted by a sentimental man looking back on the trials of fleeting youth.

(It is interesting to me that the scene in Miyazaki's *Howl's Moving Castle* where the scarecrow takes the washing line up high is just like a scene from the Kiki novel, an episode Miyazaki didn't use for his Kiki movie.)

Diana Wynne Jones's novel *Howl's Moving Castle* is self-referential to fairytales but not so far as to be parody in the style of *The Princess Bride* or *Shrek*. Instead it offers a balancing act between the postmodern and the pre-modern.

It is one thing to have characters aware that "trolls live under bridges" or "genies grant three wishes," since these are part of the common culture within fairytales, and indeed, they give the stories the power to move the plot forward. In my opinion it is another thing entirely for a firstborn to say, "I'm doomed! I'd better play it safe based on what happened to all those other firstborns of fairytale." This threatens the entire fabric of fairytale! Granted, "triumph of the underdog" is a staple of fairytale, but still, Sophie is only an "underdog" by the reader-known rules that have somehow invaded the fairytale landscape. She is a victim of a metafictional institution.

Miyazaki's *Howl's Moving Castle* seems to me to borrow some of the steampunk flavor of Pullman's *The Golden Compass* in painting Sophie's world. In Diana Wynne Jones's novel, the talk of war made me think in terms of medieval fighting: bows, horses, swords, and maybe crossbows (but I doubted that). In Miyazaki's movie the war arrives and we go from Victorian Era to late World War Two city bombing in jiff time.

THE CHALLENGER:
SATOSHI KON

KON CAPSULES

A Quick Guide to "Anime's Hitchcock"

Millennium Actress created a buzz with its world premiere at Fantasia Festival 2001 in Canada. The second movie from Satoshi Kon, it was said to be beautiful, challenging, and haunting, perhaps an invasion from "art house" into mainstream.

Relatively unknown on both sides of the Pacific, Kon was born and raised in Hokkaido, the northern island of Japan. He went to Tokyo as an outsider and maintained an aloof attitude. His artistic vision is dark, cold, and scary, but there is another side, one showing miracles and redemption.

Among Kon's American fans is director Darren Aronofsky, whose award-winning *Requiem for a Dream* (2000) has a bathtub scene inspired by Kon's *Perfect Blue* (1997). Aronofsky's later Oscar-winning *Black Swan* (2010) exhibits large scale similarities to *Perfect Blue,* but this might be due to both films being in the genre of art house thriller.

Where Miyazaki got onto the Disney highway for distribution, Kon took a different route, growing his audience in Japan by starting overseas. Call it the art house byway, racking up foreign reviews and foreign awards to support a roadshow in Japan. *Perfect Blue* premiered in 1997 at overseas venues, winning awards in Canada and Portugal before its general release in Japan in 1998. As mentioned before, *Millennium Actress* debuted in Canada before being released in Japan in 2002. *Tokyo Godfathers* premiered at Big Apple Anime Fest, then appeared at San Diego Asian Film Festival, before showing in Japan in 2003. *Paprika* was at festivals in Italy, the USA, Poland, and Taiwan before its release in Japan.

The Kon Works (four motion pictures, a television series, and one short) that will be mentioned in this study:

Perfect Blue (1997)
Kon's directorial debut is a psychological thriller based upon a novel of the same name. The heroine Mima is trying to make the transition from virginal pop idol singer to serious actress, but as she goes through stages of degradation and becomes a victim of stalking, she begins to lose her grip on reality. Kon is seen as being the "Alfred Hitchcock" of anime. 1h 21m, rated R.

Millennium Actress (2001)
Set in Japan in 2001, a two-man documentary team is interviewing the elderly Chiyoko Fujiwara, a cinematic superstar who has been in reclusive hiding for 30 years. What follows is a masterpiece of interwoven tales, where fact, fiction, and film blend, merge, and cross-pollinate. 1h 27m, rated PG.

Tokyo Godfathers (2003)
An action/comedy wherein a trio of homeless people discover a crying baby in a dumpster and struggle to find justice for her. A mix of Capra's Christmas film *It's a Wonderful Life* (1946) and John Ford's Western film *3 Godfathers* (1948). 1h 32m, rated PG-13.

Paranoia Agent (2004)
A psychological-thriller television series. A bat-wielding skater is beating people at random. Police detectives find it gets weirder and weirder. 13 episodes, 25 minutes each, rated TV-14.

Paprika (2006)
Science fiction psychological thriller based upon a novel of the

same name. A high tech device for entering the dreams of others has fallen into sinister hands. 1h 30m, rated R.

Short

Magnetic Rose (1995)

A short space adventure from the anthology *Memories*. A salvage crew investigates an SOS signal in space. While Kon did not direct this one, he wrote the script (from a story by Katsuhiro Otomo), designed the characters, and did the layout. 44 minutes, rated PG-13.

FOUR KON POINTS

*"Millennium Actress" as Key to
the Work of Satoshi Kon*

(2006)

[From a video presentation given to an undergraduate class at Indiana University. They had watched Kon's *Millennium Actress* and I was using that as a springboard to talk about recurring elements in Kon's work.]

Satoshi Kon's second movie is *Millennium Actress* (2001). Through studying it we can see four elements that Kon uses repeatedly in his work: the Kon Heroine; a pair of investigators, soft and hard; a breakthrough/breakdown; and a shifting reality.

The five pieces by Kon we will examine are all of the quest type, in that the characters come out profoundly changed from the way they went in. This is different from the adventure type, where Indy Jones or Captain Kirk do not change.

Kon is essentially creating mystery films. In *Millennium Actress* the initial mystery is "Why did Chiyoko become a recluse?" The next mystery is "What does the key she was given unlock?" Kon's other works begin with mysteries: Who sent the deep space SOS? Who is killing people around the new actress? Who abandoned the baby in the trash? Who is attacking random people in

Tokyo?

Kon's mystery is always attached to a woman, and usually she is the heroine herself.

The Kon Heroine

The Kon heroine is either an artist of some kind or a pre-career girl: in *Millennium Actress* we have Chiyoko who is both a rebellious girl and the actress she becomes.

> *Scene (0:10:25): The studio head is lecturing schoolgirl Chiyoko and her mother on how being an actress in a movie set in Manchuria would cheer the Japanese soldiers stationed there and serve the nation of Japan. Her mother says Chiyoko is too timid to be an actress, and will instead marry, have children, and inherit the candy shop. Chiyoko herself is not allowed to speak.*

> *Scene (0:29:50): In a samurai movie, Chiyoko encounters a ghost hag who tells her that Chiyoko has drunk "thousand year tea," which will curse her to burn with unfulfilled love. But then the hag says, "I hate you! More than I can bear! And I love you! More than I can bear!" With a final cackle, the ghost disappears.*

Note how Chiyoko's struggle with the ghost is a conflict between her past and future self.

Magnetic Rose is a short space adventure (44 minutes) from the anthology *Memories* (1995). Kon did not direct this one, but since he wrote the script, designed the characters, and did the layout, his influence on it is profound. In *Magnetic Rose* the heroine is Eva the opera diva.

> *Scene (18:00): The spaceman Miguel is admiring a photograph of the mysterious woman in red, before a wall hung*

with many photos of her. He asks, "Is she an actress or something? Wouldn't you say so, Heinz?" Heinz, in an adjacent trophy room, reports she is an opera singer.

Note the actress/singer connection that Miguel makes.

Perfect Blue (1997) was Kon's directorial debut and is based upon a novel of the same name. The heroine Mima has been a virginal pop idol, but she is trying to make the transition from singer to actress. Here are two clips to show the conflict.

> *Scene (0:02:40): Mima, standing in a moving train car, begins little dance moves; dissolve to a performance where she and her two singing girlfriends won the enthusiastic response of a young male audience; dissolve to Mima buying groceries at a market.*

> *Scene (0:28:42): Mima is at a table, studying a movie script. A man is telling her agent about it, wherein Mima's character goes through a profound change after being raped at a strip club. The agent, a middle-aged woman, is appalled at the idea of her client being in a rape scene. She tells Mima not to worry, that she will get the producer to change it. But Mima says she will do it, as part of her own change from idol to actress. The agent is stunned.*

Notice how the confrontation between the heroine and authority figures prefigures the parallel confrontation in *Millennium Actress*.

After *Millennium Actress*, Kon wrote and directed *Tokyo Godfathers* (2003). Miyuki is the rebellious girl who has run away from home, now living on the streets with two bums.

> *Scene (0:04:08): While the bums are sorting through trash, one starts lecturing Miyuki. She responds with violence. They begin to fight, only stopping when they hear the cries of a baby from the trash nearby.*

Note that while she is not the baby's mother, Miyuki acts as a thematic double in that she has abandoned her family.

Paranoia Agent (2004) is Kon's TV series, running thirteen episodes. Tsukiko is a character designer who dreams up mascot-like figures that are replicated in cartoons, games, and toys. This is Kon poking at the manga-anime industrial complex of Japan.

> *Scene from episode 1 (3:34): Tsukiko is having a creative block on designing the next cute character. The pressure is on for another hit like her last one, the pink dog Maromi.*

> *Scene (5:05): As Tsukiko walks home late at night, talking to her plush toy Maromi, she surprises a bag lady digging in the trash. Tsukiko hurries past the woman, but when she looks back, the other has vanished and an eerie darkness begins coming down the street toward her. In panic she turns and runs.*

Notice how Tsukiko's encounter with the bag lady echoes Chiyoko's seeing the ghost: they menace and then disappear.

Two Investigators

Every mystery needs an investigator, and usually Kon uses two: one who is hard and the other who is soft. (The exception is in *Perfect Blue,* where the heroine is also the investigator.)

In *Millennium Actress,* Ida the cameraman is the hard investigator who has no emotional investment in the project, while his boss, Genya, is the soft one since he is a lifelong fan of the actress.

In *Magnetic Rose* the Germanic spaceman Heinz, a married man, is the hard realist, while Latin Miguel the womanizer is the soft romantic.

In *Tokyo Godfathers* the straight bum Gin is the hard realist and the gay bum Hana is the soft romantic.

In *Paranoia Agent* the investigators are police detectives. Ikari (married) is the "bad cop" hard one and his partner Maniwa (single) is the "good cop" soft one.

Breakthrough

In the course of a Kon mystery there is a point where the hard investigator seems to experience a breakthrough into a new reality, which might also be a mental breakdown. In *Millennium Actress* this moment comes when hard Ida the cameraman sees the bandits attacking the derailed Manchurian train.

> *Scene (0:25:53): Ida shouts, "Hey! This is really happening!" Running through the burning car, he cries to Genya, "Boss! Let's get out of here!"*

In *Magnetic Rose* we see hard Heinz deal with it.

> *Scene (28:55): Heinz is enjoying a cup of coffee at home with his wife and their young daughter. Suddenly the flowers on the table start writhing, and when Heinz stands up in alarm, his wife changes into Eva the diva, saying that he cannot leave. Color bleeds out of the room, which is revealed to be just a movie set.*

In *Perfect Blue*, Mima is on her own.

> *Scene (0:39:00): Mima is trapped in a room, arguing with a computer that has her "old self" as idol. After berating Mima for being tarnished as a filthy actress, the old self steps forth into the room as a glowing ghost.*

In *Tokyo Godfathers* all the investigators are finally on the same page, if only for a moment.

> *Scene (0:57:32): The two bums are sitting at the little booth in the front of a convenience store late at night, try-*

ing to soothe the crying baby. The store clerk asks them to leave, and a drunk customer begins to berate them. The group moves outside and the confrontation becomes physical, until it is interrupted by an ambulance crashing into the shop—they would have all been killed if they were still there. Hana sums it up, "I knew it! Kiyoko [the baby] really is the messenger of God!"

By episode five of *Paranoia Agent*, the detectives finally have a suspect in custody only after the mysterious bat-wielding attacker has struck several more victims. They question him in an attempt to determine if he is the original perpetrator or a copycat, but his story seems based upon a heroic fantasy computer game.

Scene from episode 5 (8:43–9:00): The hard inspector is inside of a computer game, terrified by the monster that the teenage suspect dispatches with cool efficiency.

Shifting Realities

Kon's works for cinema and TV are all about shifting realities. To avoid ruining the others for viewers who have not yet seen them, we will now focus entirely on *Millennium Actress*.

The initial reality of *Millennium Actress* is that of a documentary, or perhaps more specifically, the making of a documentary. When we see what the camera sees we are lured into thinking that we are watching objective reality.

The Hat Trick

But a magical subjectivity creeps in, beginning with that early scene showing the argument between Chiyoko's mother and the movie studio executive. Later in that first "mini-breakthrough" sequence, Chiyoko runs in AD 1940 to catch the train and loses her hat. Genya seems to catch the hat (0:18:38) within the subjective frame, but Ida reacts with surprise seeing the hat in his hands (0:20:33) in the objective frame of AD 2000: we are led to believe that this hat magically materialized as Chiyoko told her compelling story; or that they were involved in real time travel.

Mystical Level

In the same sequence that begins with Ida's breakthrough on the train (0:25:53), Chiyoko runs into a historical movie set in AD 1500, where she sees the wraith and drinks the thousand-year tea. This seems to represent a mystical level of more potent magic.

The Second Hat Trick

After Ida's big breakthrough with the bandits shooting the train, we would expect him to be respectful of the magic going on around him. But that sequence ends with a double deflation.

First we see "what the camera sees," which is two people re-enacting movie scenes in a living room (0:32:22). This is a stunning reversal of the whole train experience.

Then we see the second "hat trick," where Genya hands his samurai helmet to the maid (0:32:40), which suggests that she is perhaps supplying them, too. The magic is completely dispelled.

Jaded

But no, the magic is still there: we come to realize that Ida accepts it but does not respect it. He is jaded and pokes fun at it when Chiyoko runs from Edo of AD 1500 to Kyoto of the twentieth century, even as he is drawn into stronger magic.

> Scene (0:37:26): Chiyoko the geisha is captured and pulled away for discipline; Ida makes a new establishing shot and says, "Now we're in Kyoto [. . .] faster than a speeding bullet train! Another age, too."

Recent History a Cipher

Ida's supposed objectivity comes into question when we discover that he cannot recognize the reality of seeing a firebombed Tokyo of AD 1944.

Scene (0:47:40): Young Chiyoko, wearing the WWII bomb-shielding hood and short cape, is walking through the Tokyo ruins when air sirens wail. Searchlights wave and a bomber armada fills the sky. Ida says, "Wow, is this science fiction?" to which Genya snaps, "Idiot!"

After this we might ask, "What sort of fantasy passes for reality among the post-war generations of Japan?" More pressing is the fact that our "reality anchor" has been severed; hard Ida is revealed to be unreliable.

Home on the Stage
Here is a further collapse of rules.

Scene (1:00:50): Housewife Chiyoko is dusting the study while a TV reports on recent American manned spaceflight. A pile of books tumble, and among them she finds a box with her lost key in it. Her husband enters and she shows it to him in mute accusation. Suddenly stage lights are turned off—what seemed to be a study is revealed to be merely a movie set. Eiko, Chiyoko's nemesis, appears and says, "Well, now she knows." Eiko then confesses to her part in stealing the key in order to push Chiyoko toward marrying the director.

What must be a real life domestic discovery and argument is morphed onto a movie set. This is simply not possible. It reverses causality of what happened when the key was lost: at that time they were filming a movie (the one where a mother tries to convince her daughter to take an arranged marriage) and after the camera stopped the disappearance of the key set off a fruitless search. Here the key is found and the scene blends seamlessly into a rehearsal for a movie scene, but the initial discovery continues in a non-scripted way with the arrival of Eiko.

Note how the morphing into a movie set is an echo from Heinz's earlier breakthrough in *Magnetic Rose*, where his familiar home became an alien set.

The Mystical Level

All of these breakdowns prepare us to accept the mystical level as being perhaps the most valid: that Chiyoko, through reincarnations, has been chasing after the key man for 500 years (the setting of her Warring States movies) and will continue to chase for 500 more (the setting of "Planet Zed").

MILLENNIUM ACTRESS APPENDIX

Timeline, Made-up Movies,
The Human Condition

Timeline

1915   Ginei Studios founded.
1923   Chiyoko born during Kanto earthquake.
1932   Manchukuo.
1937   Sino-Japanese War begins; Chiyoko is 14.
1940   Chiyoko is 17, makes first movie this year (book).*
1941   Sneak attack at Pearl Harbor.
1945   Firebombing, end of war; Chiyoko is 22.
1948   Studio recovers, Chiyoko becomes star (book).*
1953   Chiyoko is 30.
1958?   Chiyoko loses key and gets married.
1962   "Friendship 7" launches; Chiyoko finds lost key.
1963   Chiyoko is 40.
1970   Chiyoko goes into hiding at 47.
1985   Ginei Studios closes, 70 years after being founded.
2000?   Ginei Studios demolished.

* "Book" here being *Chiyoko: Millennial Actress (Special Edition)*. Tokyo: Madhouse, 2002.

Documentary

The title of Genya's documentary is "The Seven Specters: the Legend of Fujiwara Chiyoko" (38:24), which turns out to be a play on the film title *Chiyoko no ninpou shichihenge* ("The Seven Disguises of Ninja Chiyoko"). Genya's poster for the documentary suggests that he considers Chiyoko's seven greatest roles to be:

1. Red Cross Girl—from *Shoui no yushi,* her first film.

2. Bonnet girl in Meiji era, set circa 1870s.

3. Bicycle girl with big red bow and hakama, set circa 1900s.

4. Princess—from *Kurenai no hana* ("Deep Red Flower").

5. Ninja—from *Chiyoko no ninpou shichihenge* ("The Seven Disguises of Ninja Chiyoko").

6. Geisha—from *Shimabara junjou* ("Shimabara Pureheart").

7. Astronaut—from *Yusei Z* ("Planet Zed"), her last film.

There are no hints as to the titles or themes of the films with "bonnet girl" and "bicycle girl," seen in the "riding woman" montage (0:42:28–0:43:38), but it seems likely that they were made before 1945, perhaps even during the war period 1942–45. The "bicycle girl" story seems to involve a former rickshaw man repaying the kindness of an aristocratic young woman.

Chiyoko's Major Movies

Millennium Actress shows a lot of movie magazines on Chiyoko's coffee table, as well as movie posters glimpsed on the walls at the movie studio itself. One of the fascinating details in the book *Chiyoko: Millennial Actress* is a filmography of Chiyoko's major movies, giving a poster and a synopsis for each of seventeen titles. I have augmented this material with title translations, a guess for the release years in square brackets (based on the order of the films and clues in the text), location of the film reference within *Millennium Actress,* and commentary.

.

Shoui no yushi ("Wounded Soldiers") [1940 given in text]. Synopsis: "An army lieutenant saves Chiyoko from a gang of hoodlums. To see him again, she travels to China as a Red Cross nurse. However, because of his involvement in military intelligence, she is unable to track him down. Her path is fraught with many perils. She endures an invasion by bandits. A wealthy Manchurian threatens her chastity. A mysterious female spy appears and interferes with her. This film is her debut, filmed before World War II."

Location: (0:22:58–0:23:27) filming scene.

Commentary: Chiyoko's first film, included as one of Genya's "seven greatest" list.

Kimi o shitaite ("I Pine for You") [circa 1947]. Synopsis: "Chiyoko secretly meets her lover despite the marriage that her mother is arranging for her. However, thinking of her happiness, her lover decides to leave her and head for Manchuria. The farewell scene at the train station drives the audience to tears. When this movie was released, the painful memories of war were still present in the audience."

Location: (0:19:58–0:20:07) missing the train; (0:20:30) movie poster.

Commentary: The "missing the train" tableau comes after the first "running woman" sequence. This clip is the first to be shown in Chiyoko's narrative, but it is not from her first film; it is from the film that was probably her fourth.

Ayakashi no shiro ("Ayakashi Castle") [circa 1950]. Synopsis: "Set in feudal Japan, Chiyoko plays a princess traveling to a neighboring country to be wed. During her travels, she spots a handsome young man playing a flute. Unknown to her, he is her future husband. However, before the marriage can take place, his father dies under suspicious circumstances. This was perpetrated by a mysterious old woman that was rumored to be living in the castle tower for a long time. The day the prince was to inherit the crown, the subjects stage a revolt. This film combines ghostly tales with romance."

Location: (0:26:54–0:31:24) burning castle and encounter with ghost.

Commentary: Writers often link this one to Kurosawa's *Throne of Blood* (1957).

Kurenai no hana ("Deep Red Flower") [circa 1955]. Synopsis: "A concubine, portrayed by Eiko, conspires with the lord's subjects and stages a revolt. They kidnap the lord to find out the location of buried gold. His princess, determined to rescue the lord, disguises herself as a brave young soldier and sets out to save him. Chiyoko's bravery, combined with the unrequited love and loyalty for Chiyoko by her faithful, family servant, touches the heart of the audience. This fantastic film celebrates the 40th anniversary of Ginei Studios."

Location: (0:31:25–0:32:16) riding horses with Nagato.

Commentary: This clip transitions from the burning castle movie with a sudden costume change. Number four on Genya's "seven greatest" list. Genya plays a supporting role in the reenactment.

Chiyoko no ninpou shichihenge ("The Seven Disguises of Ninja Chiyoko") [circa 1957]. Synopsis: "Just like the title, this film is a historical musical that has Chiyoko turning into seven different characters, including a city girl, a female ninja, and a male wanderer, among others. Her grandfather informs her that she is a descendant of the Koga Ninjas. Using the ninja tricks described in her family ninja scroll, she sets off to rescue her falsely accused lover. This film was made in the late 1950s. Although Chiyoko was in her 30s by the time she played this role, her youthful features allowed her to credibly play a role of a young maiden."

Location: (0:33:02–0:36:30) the pilgrim Chiyoko tries to free a prisoner being transported.

Commentary: Number five in Genya's list of "seven greatest." Curiously, among the five disguises shown on the movie poster is one that looks very much like the warrior princess of *Kurenai no hana.*

Shimabara junjou ("Shimabara Pureheart"). Synopsis: "Set in the Shimabara district of Kyoto, Eiko plays a geisha that has shown Chiyoko the ropes of the trade. Eiko becomes increasingly jealous as Chiyoko's popularity exceeds her own, and she also becomes vexed at Chiyoko's honest nature. Despite the custom that discourages geishas from seeing their clients outside of their business, Chiyoko falls in love with a client, and tries to see him outside of work. The film touches on the subject of the women's liberation movement after the war. Portraying the struggles of an independent woman, Chiyoko's character attracted sympathy from the audience."

Location: (0:36:31–0:37:22) Chiyoko is shoved to the floor by Eiko; (0:37:51–0:38:25) Chiyoko, beaten, is lectured by Eiko; (0:38:47–0:39:22) Chiyoko is set free by Genya.

Commentary: Number six in Genya's list of seven.

Yuki no zesshou ("Song of Snow"). Synopsis: "Set during the revolutionary period before the end of the Edo government in Japan, this period piece centers on a tragic love story between a city girl and an escaped soldier. The backdrop of heavy snow works to enhance the romantic mood throughout the film. Chiyoko is trying to reunite with her lover held as a political prisoner by counterrevolutionaries. However, Chiyoko faces interference by the arrival of a mysterious woman, played by Eiko. The mysterious woman works as a geisha at night, and also works as a spy against revolutionaries from escaped soldiers to the counterrevolutionaries. She also nurses a deep hatred toward Chiyoko's father."

Location: (0:39:41–0:41:47) escaped prisoner, snow.

Commentary: This clip is very much like the biographical episode where Chiyoko met the Man with the Key.

Kaiketsu kuro tengu ("The Extraordinary Black Tengu"). Synopsis: "Number six in The Extraordinary Black Tengu series, starring the popular actor Kanjuro Oishi, this is his most popular role.

Set in Kyoto during the later Edo dynasty, this series portrays the battle between the hero, Kuro Tengu, and the supporters of the Shogun. Known for casting popular actors as guest stars, [the series brought in Chiyoko] . . . as the guest star for the sixth episode. Chiyoko is planning to help her childhood friend, who has been captured by right wing extremists. The Kuro Tengu secretly comes to her aid. Love and romance are woven into the plot, which makes it an unusual episode for a series targeted toward adolescent boys."

Location: (0:41:47–0:42:27) action hero whistles up a horse.

Commentary: Genya is playing the star of this film, where Chiyoko is the guest star. This movie invades the previous one when Genya drops into the scene from above. At the end of the clip Chiyoko gallops into the "riding woman" montage, with a cameo of "bonnet girl" and scenes of "bicycle girl," caping a medley of five melded movies.

Meguri ai ("Together by Chance") [circa 1960]. Synopsis: "A classic drama centered on chance meetings, it was made into a successful movie starring Chiyoko Fujiwara, and Keizo Sahara, a popular contract actor with Ginei Studios."

Location: (0:52:21–0:52:26) Chiyoko steps into the embrace and the scene forms the movie poster.

Commentary: This title was used as the Japanese name for *An Affair to Remember* (1957), which makes it difficult to come up with a plausible alternative.

Tokyo no madonna ("Tokyo Madonna"). Synopsis: "Chiyoko plays a bus guide. Both she and the bus driver like each other but cannot confess their feelings to each other. The bus driver's father and the younger brother of Chiyoko's character hassle them with unwanted advice. The conflict between Chiyoko's modern character and the bus driver's older sister (played by Eiko) gives the movie flavor."

Location: (0:56:14–0:56:22) billboard of movie.

Commentary: No scenes are shown, but the term "madonna"

is used in a mother/daughter conversation that morphs into a scene (0:57:12–0:57:19) of another movie, the film *Onna no niwa*.

Manabiya no haru ("Springtime at the Academy"). Synopsis: "Chiyoko plays a teacher transferred to an all-girl academy. Using the Shinshu area as a backdrop for this emotional tale, the film centers around Chiyoko and her relationships with her students. Chiyoko's vivid speech and action breathe fresh air into the conservative institution. However, this offends some students' parents. The scene where Chiyoko is leaving after being fired from the school drives the audience to tears."

Location: (0:59:09–0:59:42) teacher at blackboard.

Manatsu no suiheisen ("Midsummer Horizon"). Synopsis: "Chiyoko plays a daughter of a wealthy family that arrives in Zushi Beach. Soon, she is courted by three men. Masaya the playboy, Sakai the intellectual, and Kishikawa the kind and quiet man, all court her for her affections. Who will finally win her heart?"

Location: none. Possible "behind the scenes" vignettes for this movie include Genya's first day on the job at the beach (0:53:27) and the beach house seduction (0:54:36–0:55:50), but the balcony room has posters for *Onna no niwa* and *Kaseki no ie* (0:55:38), making it less a "movie set" and more a chronological challenge.

Commentary: No scenes are shown, but the mother/daughter conversation that morphs into a scene (0:57:12–0:57:19) from *Onna no niwa* begins with Chiyoko rejecting the glossy photos of three prospective "arranged marriage" suitors.

Onna no niwa ("Women's Garden") [circa 1958]. Synopsis: "It portrays the generational gap and the resulting struggles between a mother and daughter. The mother, in her past, agreed to an arranged marriage but is unable to forget her true love. The daughter, nursing an unrequited love, struggles to remain single. During the filming, Chiyoko was already in her mid-thirties. It is ironic considering the content of the film, but Chiyoko marries [director]

Otaki soon after the release of the film."

Location: (0:57:12–0:57:19) filming scene that is used for poster.

Commentary: Notice that in Chiyoko's wedding photo (1:00:05), her mother is represented by a framed photo held by a mature woman.

Kaseki no ie ("House of Fossils"). Synopsis: "A controversial piece by [director] Junichi Otaki that examines happiness in life and the meaning of family. Chiyoko's character is a woman finally finding contentment with a happy marriage and a child. Suddenly, the father that had abandoned her as a child shows up at her doorstep with her much younger sister."

Location: none.

Commentary: Possibly the "house study" set Chiyoko is cleaning (1:00:05) is a set for this movie.

Torakku taishou ("Taisho Trucking") [circa 1964]. Synopsis: "This is one of the most popular series starring Takahara Genta, who is known for his yakuza roles. He plays a trucker who is undefeated in fighting, but is constantly getting his heart broken by women. In every episode, he falls in love with a woman during his travels, and inevitably gets his heart broken. In this episode, Chiyoko plays a beautiful city girl traveling to forget about her ex-lover. Although the trucker falls in love with her, knowing that her heart belongs to an ex-lover, he helps her find her way back to her lover."

Location: (1:09:00–1:09:13) on the highway, a semi-truck stops.

Commentary: Again, Genya is the star and Chiyoko is the guest star.

Gigalla [circa 1968]. Synopsis: "Ginei Studios' first monster movie during the height of the monster movie explosion. The mutant result of a nuclear explosion, Gigalla is immune to any weapons known to man. Chiyoko, playing a female scientist, tries to recruit a senior scientist, played by Eiko, in her fight to find an effective weapon. She feels that the new drug that Eiko has been developing might be the key to defeating Gigalla. However, Eiko unjustly blames Chiyoko for a lab accident that has left her scarred from burns, and refuses to help Chiyoko."

Location: (0:52:31–0:52:34) promotional event; (1:09:30–1:09:40) scenes.

Yusei Z ("Planet Zed") [circa 1970]; heroine an astronaut/scientist. Synopsis: "This is a sci-fi film made after the success of *Gigalla*. A group of scientists is trying to prevent a huge meteor from crashing into earth by taking advantage of distortions in space to send the meteor into a black hole. Chiyoko travels alone into the black hole to rescue her lover, who went into the black hole first. This was Chiyoko's final film, and she actually disappeared from the studio during the making of this film. The film was completed using a substitute actress."

Location: (0:00:16–0:01:38) opening scene of *Millennium Actress;* (1:10:36–1:11:07) filming interrupted by earthquake; (1:12:46–1:13:48) Genya reenacts; (1:21:01–1:22:25) Chiyoko's farewell.

Commentary: Genya's number seven of Chiyoko's seven greatest roles. This is the film Genya is watching in the opening scene.

Book
Chiyoko: Millennial Actress (Special Edition). Tokyo: Madhouse, 2002.

·

The Likely Debt of Millennium Actress to Kobayashi's Human Condition Trilogy
It appears that Kon's cinephilic sensation owes something to an art house giant.

Masaki Kobayashi's Human Condition trilogy (1959/61) is 579 minutes long. Set during World War Two, it is about a Japanese pacifist who navigates a path through the war, becoming by turns a labor camp supervisor in Manchuria (the first film), an army conscript fighting against the Soviets in China (the second film), and a prisoner of war in the USSR (the third film).

These movies provide a remarkably frank view of Imperial Japan's rough behavior in China. While some elements, such as the separation of the couple by the war, and the visit to Japanese occupied Manchuria, might be reasonably considered as elements generic to the scenario, there is one thing Satoshi Kon took from this monumental epic and applied repeatedly to *Millennium Actress,* that being the endless march homeward in the third film, which Kon transforms into Chiyoko's endless running, trudging toward her missing lover.

No Greater Love (1959)
Road to Eternity (1959)
A Soldier's Prayer (1961)

GODFATHERS: THE BRIGHT SIDE OF KON

(2021)

I suspect that Kon's *Tokyo Godfathers* gets at Ford's *3 Godfathers* entirely through the manga *Seraphim: 266613336 Wings* by Mamoru Oshii and Kon. In a nutshell, Ford's movie is about cowboys fighting Nature to transport a newborn, whereas the manga is about agents passing across a fractured China to deliver a teen. Through drawing the manga, Kon learned not only about the bible's three Magi, but also about angels, since the "seraphim" of the title are a type of angel. Because the manga was unfinished, Kon was presumably left with a lot of unused ideas, and it looks to me like he reworked it all: converting the UN agents into homeless bums; scaling down the petty states of a future China into the districts of Tokyo; and adding "angels" in such varied places as a billboard, a cat's name, and a drag venue.

To that rough-yet-accurate outline I add further details from more of Kon's manga. The biggest case is "Joyful Bell" (1989), a Christmas story where a fake Santa tries to deliver a lost girl to her home across Tokyo. This proves Kon had the germ of *Tokyo Godfathers* in 1989 (a Christmas-time adventure comedy; a lost child; an episodic journey across the city; and benevolent supernatural elements), the main changes being a swapping out of the fake Santa for the dubious Magi, and making the mystery child a newborn (in the style of *3 Godfathers*). Two of Kon's other manga show traces of influence: Hana's haiku pronouncements find a root in

"The Adventures of Master Basho" (1989); and the action sequence with the truck at the end is anticipated in "Kidnappers" (1987) with a "struggle at the door of a moving vehicle" scene, and a "kick-off from the vehicle about to plow into a storefront" scene.

From the genre of traditional Christmas movies, I detect shades of "A Christmas Carol" in the fact that alcoholic Gin sees his future self in the old dying man, meets a more successful present self in the doctor, and grapples with his past self in Sachiko's gambling-addict husband, all a nod to Ebenezer Scrooge seeing his past, present, and future.

Tokyo Godfathers is a Christmas story where Christmas really drives the story: watching the nativity play leads Hana to use the "eating for two" gag (when Hana had always wanted to get an extra portion for the absent Miyuki); Hana's Christmas present for Miyuki as lost books in the trash heap leads to the fight where Hana says, "Not on Christmas," emphasizing that the sacred nature of the date is well-known to these non-Christians; Hana's name of "Kiyoko" for the baby is derived from the "Silent Night" song they had heard (clipping the title "Kiyoshi Kono Yoru"); Miyuki's purchase of bottled water is so stunning to the cashier that Miyuki calls it a "Christmas Miracle"; et cetera. Then there is the oft-reported use of "12–25," the calendar date for Christmas, in various details: the locker number "1225" on the key found with the baby (0:06:17); the Club Swirl business cards with phone number ending "1225" (0:17:31) and the street address "12-2-5" (0:24:45); the taxi cab licence plate "12-25" (0:29:34); the cab fare "12,250" yen (0:42:05); the stopped clock "12:25" (0:53:11) and the new address written on the calendar "1-2-25" (0:54:16).

Kon uses the difficult trick of getting the audience to see the miracles that the characters do not recognize. This starts right after they take up the baby: a falling bucket of paint barely misses hitting them; then, when Hana stops to argue, a skidding vehicle knocks down a couple in the crosswalk where Hana would have been. Much later in the film, when this vehicular-impact gag is repeated by the ambulance slamming into the convenience store, the three Magi are willing to admit it is a miracle.

The biblical Magi brought gold, frankincense, and myrrh as their presents to baby Jesus. Gin's name suggests precious metals (the "gin" of "ginko," meaning "bank"), and he is the one who receives the winning lottery ticket. In a weaker case, "Hana" can mean "flower," which might allude to frankincense and myrrh, since both are aromatic, but both come from trees rather than flowers. Miyuki's name gives no hints. She is associated with angels (used for billboard, cat, and drag venue), but Angel Tower is also Hana's home. Where Gin's sin is Gambling and Hana's sin is Wrath, Miyuki's sin is Violence, making her a perfect match for the beagle Magi in the manga *Seraphim,* a canine with the unexpected superpower of super-violence.

Gin seems more central to the story than the other two Magi. His lies (that he was a bicycle racer; that his daughter and wife died) become true (he races on a bike to catch the truck at the end; the doctor who is like his twin brother actually did lose his daughter and wife to death). The two weddings, the yakuza one in the present and the nurse one in the near future, are both related to Gin. The repetitions of the name "Kiyoko" (for foundling, yakuza bride, cell phone party-girl, and daughter-nurse) all relate to Gin.

Gin seems a bit like Odysseus at such moments as the scene where he is with the dying man, a case where he can only leave after administering the powerful alcohol he had picked up in an earlier adventure, just the way that Odysseus escaped the cave of the Cyclops. And the journey of the travelers across Tokyo is truly an "odyssey" regarding the colorful societal "islands" they pass through as they try to find "home" for the baby and even themselves.

But the Dante pattern is stronger: first the party visits a cemetery, then they help an underworld lord and are welcomed into an underworld palace. Here the party is split up, yet by their separate trials of blood, sweat, and tears, they are reunited at the heavenly Angel Tower, a clear movement from the underworld to the overworld.

They return to the middle ground to continue their quest. In the end Hana flies like an angel, saving the precious baby.

Kon showed great daring in selecting homeless people to be the heroes of his film, and further verve in suggesting at the end that each of the three can go home again.

I see a lot of deep Christian content in this motion picture. The moment when the scavengers find the baby, they go through a shock that recalls the thief who was crucified next to Jesus:

> *One of the criminals who hung there hurled insults at him: "Aren't you the Messiah? Save yourself and us!"*

> *But the other criminal rebuked him. "Don't you fear God," he said, "since you are under the same sentence? We are punished justly; for we are getting what our deeds deserve. But this man has done nothing wrong." (Luke 23: 39–41; NIV)*

That is, the thief says, "We deserve to be in such a wretched position because of our actions, but Jesus has no guilt." In a similar way, the three homeless people seem to say the same about themselves in contrast to the baby. As such, they begin to recognize their own culpability in their current situation.

On their trail from the trash-heap, the team encounters a yakuza boss, a pimp, a hitman, a gambling-addict, and a prostitute-turned-babysnatcher. All of these are considered socially unclean. Jesus himself famously ate with tax collectors, prostitutes, and other sinners, all considered unclean. How remarkable a movie scene, then, is the case of the yakuza groom: a pimp who talks about Sachiko as an object; a bookie who was the cause of Gin's financial ruin; and a suitor who is doubted by his boss, the bride's father. This man under maximum viewer animosity, a target of Gin's righteous wrath, sacrificially takes several bullets intended for his boss/future father-in-law! And then Gin, from towering rage, drops to his knees to ask after the health of the wounded man.

The scene near the end of the movie where Gin tearfully sacrifices his "Kiyoko cash" to pay Hana's medical bill, and then receives the unexpected blessing of meeting Kiyoko herself, brings to mind two pieces of scripture about giving:

> *But this I say, He which soweth sparingly shall reap also sparingly; and he which soweth bountifully shall reap also bountifully. (2 Corinthians 9:6; KJV)*

and

> *"Bring the whole tithe into the storehouse, that there may be food in my house. Test me in this," says the Lord Almighty, "and see if I will not throw open the floodgates of heaven and pour out so much blessing that there will not be room enough to store it." (Malachi 3:10; NIV)*

This last one seems especially appropriate since the winning lottery ticket will "throw open the floodgates of heaven" for the four heroes (including the baby) in the materialistic sense of fabulous wealth.

Finally, *Tokyo Godfathers* is the most Kon-centric of Kon's work: *Perfect Blue* and *Paprika* were based upon novels; *Paranoia Agent* was built up from scraps; and *Millennium Actress* was commissioned.

.

Tokyo Godfathers: Chapters and Notes

1. Start: From a Nativity play to finding a baby in the trash heap.

2. Guardians for a Night

3. Gin's Past: He lies like Odysseus.

4. Second Thoughts

5. The Key: The key to a coin locker leads to the first clues.

6. Something Smells: They ditch the "dead" train.

7. The Cemetery: They resupply with offerings left in a cemetery.

8. Blocking a Public Thoroughfare: The yakuza boss pinned by his car feels like an allusion to that scene in *The Wizard of Oz* where Dorothy's house has landed on top of the wicked witch, an impression strengthened by the participation of a dog named "Dorothy."

9. His Daughter's Wedding: The boss's daughter is another "Kiyoko."

10. "Her Name's Sachiko": On the classical mythology side, this seems like information gained from a shade in a palace in Hades.

11. Kidnapped: Miyuki and the baby are taken by the hitman.

12. "We're Not Action-Movie Heroes": Gin halts, Hana presses on.

13. Last Request: Gin encounters an elderly double, has a Cyclops Cave adventure.

14. The Nursing Station: Fresh milk for the baby.

15. New Year's Cleanup: Punks beat Gin until another Kiyoko calls.

16. Miyuki's Past: The runaway confesses her sin to a woman who can't understand Japanese.

17. Lost Children Found: Hana locates Miyuki and the baby; they walk to Angel Tower.

18. Hana's Past: Hana confesses and regains a connection to home.

19. The Neighbors Remember

20. A Child Never Forgets Its Parents: Miyuki tries to phone home, but finds she cannot speak; the miracle of the ambulance crash.

21. Gin's Daughter: Gin sacrifices his money for Hana's medical bill and regains a connection to home in meeting his daughter Kiyoko, a nurse.

22. The Weeping Red Devil

23. Sachiko: Hana and Miyuki save Sachiko from attempted suicide, then give the baby to her.

24. Sachiko's Husband: Gin finds the truth; the three heroes save the baby; Miyuki regains a connection to home in meeting her father.

Books

Kon, Satoshi. *Dream Fossil.* (Contains the manga "Joyful Bell," "Kidnappers," and "The Adventures of Master Basho.") Vertical, 2015.

Oshii, Mamoru (author) and Satoshi Kon (illustrator). *Seraphim: 266613336 Wings.* Dark Horse Manga, 2015.

KON EXPLORES THE INSANITY OF JAPAN

[through *"Paranoia Agent"* and *"Millennium Actress"*]

(2010: The Internet Review of Science Fiction)

From its electrifying opening sequence, Satoshi Kon's animated TV series *Paranoia Agent* (2004, *Mousou dairinin*) signals that it will be about widespread insanity. With Susumu Hirasawa's exulting techno music driving it, the sequence shows a dozen characters laughing hysterically in stressful surroundings: a young woman holding her shoes stands on the top of a skyscraper, obviously on the verge of jumping; two boys stand knee-deep in the flooded remains of their shattered neighborhood; a teenage girl stands among fish under the sea; a young detective falls through the sky like a bomb released from a plane; a sleazy private investigator laughs into his cell phone in the swampy ruins of a bombed-out city; and more, reaching a climax with an older detective on a radio tower with a mushroom cloud roiling behind him. Linking them all together is a demonic rollerblading boy with a bent aluminum baseball bat ready to strike: he is "Lil' Slugger" (Shonen

Bat), the mysterious agent of paranoia.

The series begins simply enough as a detective story when a career woman named Tsukiko is the victim of an attack by a bat-wielding schoolboy on inline skates. Two police detectives are assigned to the case, and they sense that Tsukiko is hiding something, perhaps even making up the attack in order to get out of a stressful work deadline—as a cartoon character designer, she is under tremendous pressure to create a new character to follow her big hit "Maromi," a super-cute pink dog.

But then there is a second victim, a third, and a fourth. Something is happening, but the detectives cannot tell if it is the work of a single serial criminal, or a copycat criminal of a fake crime, or a combination of real crime and multiple copycats. The situation becomes increasingly unreal, and halfway through the series the detectives are removed from the case, losing their jobs, and the episodes descend into seeming chaos. Yet this is not a Post Modern "non-mystery" mystery, and the case rolls on with a life of its own to a most satisfying conclusion.

.

Kon's work is "psychological" not only in the common sense of having the focus on characters and intense emotions, with themes of illusion, reality, and insanity, but also in a more "clinical" sense as each character works to reintegrate his or her divided psyche. The two detectives quickly determine that each victim was under a great deal of pressure prior to the attack, but each victim is strangely relieved after the attack— paradoxically, the victims seem to have been *improved* by the attacks, gaining an almost eerie peace of mind. The detectives face difficulty in solving the case because each victim has a secret that he or she will not reveal.

As the thirteen-episode series progresses, the viewer discovers that the insanity is much more widespread than initially suspected. At first it seems to be spreading like an infectious disease from the one attack, but eventually it becomes more likely that it is only an expression of a society-wide condition that existed prior to the first attack. That is, the society has been insane for decades, at least, and "Lil' Slugger" is a manifestation rather than a cause. With the first few victims the viewer wonders if there is any objective reality beyond a subjective experience, because each of the focus victims is secretly insane: the first victim's doll, a Maromi toy, talks to her when no one else is around; the fourth victim is driven by his own vanity to become a violent bully; the fifth victim is a split-personality woman living different lives by day and night; the sixth is a policeman whose dream of building a house has driven him to crime and delusion. In this manner, *Paranoia Agent* paints Tokyo as a kind of Hell on Earth, populated by harried souls tormented by inner demons, considerably darker and grimmer than in Kon's movie *Tokyo Godfathers* (2003), where Tokyo is more a benign Purgatory for a trio of homeless people getting their lives in order.

In this psychological Hell of the series there is a recurring pattern of aggressors disguising themselves as victims: characters who first play the role of attacker and then have themselves attacked so as to avert suspicion. In episode 3, schoolboy Yuuichi first wishes for the attack on the third victim, a boy whose sudden popularity threatens his own, and after this wish is granted, Yuuichi wishes for an attack on himself, so as to prove to suspicious classmates and detectives alike that he is not the attacker. (After he has been attacked, he says, "I'm not the criminal . . . I'm the victim," failing to acknowledge the vanity-driven insanity he suffered.) In episode 10 the wildly incompetent Production Manager of the Maromi cartoon show does something similar. Beginning with episode 10, the soon-to-be victims are shown saying, "It isn't my fault!" regarding problems that the viewer knows really are their fault.

At the heart of it all, the Lil' Slugger mystery that sweeps the nation is the repressed childhood memory of the first victim. When Tsukiko was a girl, she blamed the death of her real-life puppy "Maromi" on a fabricated random attacker, a boy with a baseball bat, when it was really her fault. The woman Tsukiko, besieged by both cartoon Maromi and Lil' Slugger, is finally forced in the end to confront her past, at which point she heroically accepts responsibility for her part in the puppy's death, and she apologizes to her puppy with sincerity, which allows her divided psyche to be reintegrated.

At this point the opening sequence of *Paranoia Agent* turns out to be more than just a metaphorical allusion to widespread social insanity. The plot surprisingly delivers a literal and apocalyptic destruction of Tokyo. The trickle of Lil' Slugger's victims grows into a stream, yet the viewer still somehow holds onto the notion that this is all "just inside their heads," all confined to a fringe of society, even during the destruction of the city in the final episode. It is only afterward, with the city smoldering and bodies littering the street, that survivors and viewer alike seem to say, "What just happened?"

Kon does not linger on the suffering of a devastated Tokyo. In fact he jumps ahead two years to show that the city has been rebuilt and is back to normal. The citizens may even have better mental health than before, meaning that the destruction was a cathartic one, yet ambiguity remains: is it the true serenity that comes from facing up to the suppressed past, or just the "false serenity" that comes from being a victim of a "random" attack?

With *Paranoia Agent* Kon is blasting all of contemporary Japanese society as being insane, a national psyche torn between the "feel good" cuteness of Tsukiko's super-cute character "Maromi" and the terrifying darkness of Lil' Slugger. Both are symptoms of an event and a lie about the event. Kon reveals in the end that the repressed memories of guilt cause the guilty to assign blame to a "random" attacker, and that while the resulting victimhood causes temporary relief, it actually perpetuates the insanity because it does not address the root cause. Only by facing up to the past and apologizing for one's actions, as Tsukiko does, can a person reintegrate her schizoid psyche.

•

At a deeper level, *Paranoia Agent* hints at a collective guilt embracing all of modern Japan, but Kon leaves it unidentified, unnamed. When looking for an event that shook all of Japan, it is hard to avoid the end of the Pacific War and the dismantling of the

Japanese Empire. In the decades following Japan's defeat, Japan has come under criticism from Korea and China for whitewashing the warmongering activities of Imperial Japan.

Though his work, Kon is artistically grappling with what Karel van Wolferen famously calls Japan's "undigested past." In *The Enigma of Japanese Power* (1989), van Wolferen writes that the undigested past is a collective repressed memory built on a denial of Japan's "attempt to rule Asia and the blatant political suppression at home [in the pre-1945 era]." Van Wolferen writes,

> *War in this perspective is like an earthquake or a typhoon, an 'act of nature' that takes people by surprise. As one of Japan's most articulate intellectuals [Shuichi Kato] has written about the war in China: 'Seen from the outside, Japan appeared to be invading China with imperialist intentions. Seen from the inside, however, most political leaders felt that Japan was being dragged into the swamp of war as part of some inevitable process.'*

Van Wolferen posits that for the post-war Japanese, the War was not a conscious choice made by aggressors upon defenders; it was a non-human agency that caused Japan to suffer. There are no aggressors or defenders in this way of thinking: there are only Americans and victims. Addressing this, van Wolferen notes,

> *The general attitude towards the Pacific War is one of the best illustrations of Japanese 'victim consciousness.' Nearly all the war films of the past fifteen years [1974–1989] show the wartime sufferings of the Japanese people, and many young people are amazed when told that neighboring nations suffered also, possibly more, at the hands of the Japanese.*

Van Wolferen claims that the Japanese have cultivated a collective forgetting about their ruthless aggression in the nineteenth and early twentieth centuries, transforming themselves from aggressors into victims of aggression. A result of this national amnesia is an unbalanced emphasis on Japan's war sufferings, which climaxes in the viewpoint of Japan as victim of atomic bombing.

> *Mushroom clouds, it sometimes seems, have become all but mandatory in the war films made by the established Japanese studios. Here is victimhood in its ultimate guise: the atomic bombing of Hiroshima and Nagasaki. The belief in Japanese uniqueness has received very special support from these events: the Japanese did not just suffer, they suffered uniquely; one might even speak of national martyrdom.*

Van Wolferen identifies the mushroom cloud as a potent post-war symbol of Japan as victim, perhaps even the ultimate victim: a baptism by fire that erases all guilt of previous Japanese aggression.

Kon's earlier movie *Millennium Actress* (2001, *Sennen joyu*) probes these taboos regarding the War, but does so in a subtle way that avoids alarming the Japanese viewer. The heroine Chiyoko begins her acting career in 1940 with a movie filmed on location in Manchukuo, the Japanese puppet state of Manchuria that was part of Japan's attempt to rule Asia. The chief villain of *Millennium Actress* is "the Man with the Scar," an agent of the Japanese "thought police" who is pursuing Chiyoko's love interest, "the Man with the Key," showing the blatant suppression at home. It is significant that later in the movie this agent, now aged and infirm in the 1960s, appears on a personal pilgrimage to the movie studio in order to apologize to Chiyoko for his actions before the war; it is also significant that she runs away before hearing his full confession, and thus she does not learn that he murdered the Man with the Key in 1940 as she runs out to continue her quixotic quest to find him. Thus the pre-1945 period remains undigested, even for a woman who lived through it. But the Japanese viewer is insulated because this is the story of only one woman—and a rather oblivious one, at that.

In *Millennium Actress*, Kon goes so far as to directly touch on the generational-amnesia aspect of the undigested past. There is a memorable scene where Ida the cameraman, a member of the postwar generation, is magically transported back in time with his director Genya to the 1945 firebombing of Tokyo. Taking in the panorama of rubble, flames, and a sky full of heavy bombers, Ida says, "Ah, it's science fiction!" to which Genya, an older man who lived through the war, says, "You idiot." The scene is deftly done, providing some humor to lighten the grim surroundings without being too hard on Ida for his strange incomprehension about relatively recent history. In fact, Ida's condition is based on Kon himself, as he admitted in an interview: "The ignorance Ida shows regarding [wartime] history is actually a representation of me before I started working on this film [in my mid-thirties]."

Thus, Kon made his first exploration of Japan's "undigested past" in a direct but shallow way, touching on the War and its aftermath in the life of one far-from-ordinary person. In making the film he became aware of his own generational amnesia, as well.

.

According to van Wolferen, the postwar Japanese have a collective blind spot, a mental "forbidden zone" about Japanese history from around 1920 to 1945. Satoshi Kon seems to be poking at this taboo, repeatedly. In *Millennium Actress* he pokes directly but lightly, with a movie that covers the transition from pre-war to post-war: the heroine who lived through it has a strange semi-amnesia about the War and refuses to learn the truth about it; and the postwar generation cameraman has been raised in such a state of denial that he perceives it as fantasy when confronted with reality. On the other hand, in *Paranoia Agent* Kon pokes indirectly but very deeply, and while he never directly links the Japanese psychosis to the War, he does establish beyond a doubt that something happened in the past to everyone in Japan, and this something is being ignored, and now everyone is crazy.

Seen in this light, *Paranoia Agent* shows a deeper level revolving around the undigested past. Having used in the opening sequence all the potent war symbols of postwar Japan (the man falling like a bomb, the ruined city, the towering mushroom cloud), Kon suggests in the end that repressed memories of guilt (i.e., the Asia-Pacific War) cause blame to be assigned to a "random" attacker (the atom bomb), and that while the resulting victimhood causes temporary relief ("I'm not a criminal, I'm a victim"), it actually perpetuates the insanity because it does not address the root cause. Only by facing up to the undigested past (Imperial Japan's pre-1945 history) and apologizing for the nation's actions (as Tsukiko does in *Paranoia Agent*, and as the former Thought Police agent does in *Millennium Actress*) can a society reintegrate its shattered psyche.

Books

Wolferen, Karel van. *The Enigma of Japanese Power: People and Politics in a Stateless Nation.* Macmillan London, 1989.

Yokota, Masao. "Director Satoshi Kon Interview" in *Chiyoko: Millennial Actress (Special Edition)*, p. 90. Tokyo: Madhouse, 2002.

REVIEW OF PAPRIKA

*(2008: The Internet Review
of Science Fiction)*

Satoshi Kon's last film, *Paprika* (2006), is his most challenging work. It is about the DC-Mini, an experimental "dream machine" that allows a therapist to enter the dreams of her patient, and the potential for it to be misused as a weapon. Imagine an animated feature that is a reality-bending blend of Hitchcock's psychoanalytical thriller *Spellbound* (1945) and the cyberpunk movie *Strange Days* (1995), then crank it up. Because the film is so challenging, the following review will contain a lot of details that may seem like spoilers but in fact are merely enough to give readers the background and context to enjoy the movie in one viewing.

Paprika starts in the middle of a dream, where a detective is searching for a criminal at a circus. His partner seems to be a young female clown. Suddenly the circus magician performing in the center ring teleports the detective into a cage. Then the spectators in the bleachers all rush the cage, but they all have the detective's face. The ground gives way and the detective is falling through the air, but the young woman catches him while swinging by on a Tarzan vine. The pair races through several more movie scenes, chasing the fleeing criminal, before the detective wakes up in a panic.

He is in bed in a hotel room. In the other bed is the young

woman with light brown hair. She is Paprika, his new therapist. Both patient and therapist wear on their respective heads a thing that looks like a cross between a hair comb and an earpiece: the DC-Mini.

They review the dream recorded on her laptop computer. Paprika is warm, playful, and coquettish, but when the session time is up she heads for the door. He is eager to see her again because she is literally the girl of his dreams. She leaves an appointment card for him.

She exits the building and rides away on a scooter, but as she rides through the opening credits she begins to change into a different woman, a cold adult with straight black hair. This is Dr. Atsuko Chiba.

Here is the background information. Dr. Chiba, 29 years old, is a highly placed research scientist at the Foundation for Psychiatric Research. A few years earlier, her colleague, the enormously fat Dr. Tokita, invented the DC-Mini. The Foundation created a new department to deal with the device, with Tokita to handle the hardware side and Chiba to oversee the clinical trials, which were limited to simply recording the dreams of mental patients.

However, Dr. Chiba could see that Dr. Tokita was having mental troubles of his own, and so they secretly experimented, breaking protocol by sharing a dream actively as a form of therapy. This experiment was where Chiba first adopted the persona of Paprika, the 18 year old girl, while sharing the dream space of another.

Tokita quickly got over his mental trouble, making the unauthorized experiment a success. Later on, their immediate boss Dr. Shima, a dwarfish man, began suffering from depression. So Paprika helped him, too, again resulting in rapid and successful healing. The third patient of this clandestine therapy is the detective, a friend of Dr. Shima from their college days. The detective is suffering from a recurring dream and the stress of a difficult murder case.

Got all that? Good. Because when Dr. Chiba gets back to her lab at the Foundation, fat Dr. Tokita tells her they have a crisis on their hands: three DC Minis have been stolen from his office. Drs. Chiba, Tokita, and Shima have an immediate meeting to figure out what to do in order to protect their project, but the Foundation's chairman, an elderly man in a wheelchair, interrupts them.

The chairman says he already knows about the security breach. He wants to shut down the DC-Mini project. He thinks the theft they have already suffered will lead to psychic-terrorism and he wonders if the rumored person "Paprika" is behind it. The pressure is on—not only is the project threatened, but so is Paprika herself.

Suddenly Dr. Shima starts spouting nonsense, and he works himself into an enthusiasm that leads him to jump out the nearest window, high up in their multi-storied building. Luckily Shima survives his fall. They put him under observation, hooking him up to a DC-Mini, with the realization that they had witnessed the first "weaponized" use of the DC-Mini, exactly the sort of terrorism that the chairman had been talking about.

Watching the dream on the computer monitor, Dr. Chiba quickly sees that Shima has the dream of a mental patient planted in his brain. Tokita's theory is that Shima was monitoring a patient's dream during clinical trials when the terrorist used another DC-Mini to intrude, at which point the dream was projected into Shima's unconscious, where it was left like a remote-controlled bomb, waiting for the detonation signal to come. The sudden pressure of the crisis then triggered the unstable dream into taking over his waking consciousness.

Then the dream they are watching on the computer gives another clue, the appearance of fat Tokita's pudgy assistant Himuro, who spouts more of the same crazy talk that Shima had being saying during his episode. It turns out that Himuro hasn't been at the lab for a few days. He becomes the prime suspect of stealing the DC-Minis, and they go to his apartment to investigate.

There. That's the first fifteen minutes, with later details filled in for greater context. I've been careful not to ruin anything, but I'll go no further.

Fans of Kon's work know that he usually works with the

breakdown of reality. In his films *Perfect Blue* (1997) and *Millennium Actress* (2001), the tension is between the everyday world and the world of film, and how they start to blend into each other. In his TV series "Paranoia Agent" (2004) the tension is between social reality and the social unreality expressed by such things as urban legends. Kon's *Tokyo Godfathers* (2003) is softer and more subtle, being ultimately a tension between the mundane and the miraculous, which makes it the best introduction to Kon's work.

With that said, *Paprika* presents the aforementioned breakdown taken to an even higher level, to the stage where dreams and reality blend and blur. This is the heady stuff of New Wave science fiction in its heyday, from A to Z: novels like Brian Aldiss's *Barefoot in the Head* (1969), where an LSD War has left the wounded walking in a stream-of-consciousness landscape, and especially Roger Zelazny's *Dream Master* (1966), about a therapist who uses a computer to enter/experience/shape the dreams of his patients. Although it seems to come straight from the New Wave, in fact *Paprika* is based upon a Japanese science fiction novel of the same name, published in 1993. Its author is Yasutaka Tsutsui, who has a long reputation as a "New Wave" writer in Japan (with a career spanning 1965 to the present), analogous to a Kurt Vonnegut or a Philip K. Dick, but he is virtually unknown elsewhere.

Given Kon's work, *Paprika* seems like a natural for him. It is, but in a far more complicated way than just that. For starters, Kon is a long-time fan of the novel *Paprika* and admits that most of his earlier work was inspired by it. Meanwhile, Tsutsui, having seen Kon's work, decided that Kon was the one to make a movie of *Paprika*. So this is one of those rare cases where the author starts the ball rolling, participates in a small role on screen (as a bartender), and sees it through to the end.

Fans of Kon's work will find much to love in *Paprika*, a movie that starts with a bang and never lets up. Newcomers will be better prepared after reading this background information—looking over other reviews, it really bugs me that so many say that "a machine" has been stolen, when in crucial fact it is three machines that have been stolen. That seemingly innocuous simplification amounts to obfuscating misinformation.

While not for everyone, Kon's signature style of reality-breakdown is dizzying, dazzling, and delightful. Cinephiles especially are urged to give him a try.

Paprika (2006), Sony Pictures Classics. 1h 26m, rated R (for violent and sexual images). In Japanese, English-dub, French-dub, and Spanish-dub. Subtitles and bonus material, including interviews with director Kon and author Tsutsui.

PAPRIKA'S TEXT
INTO FILM

(2012)

Prior to reading Yasutaka Tsutsui's novel *Paprika* (1993), I read a number of shorter works by the author. Tsutusi has a playful style, often using fabulism. His stories frequently develop a dream-like quality—for example, one story has dream-swapping that leads to lots of dream-fornication; another story features a gritty yet absurd apocalypse as the last smoker in Japan fights for his rights in an *I Am Legend* sort of way.

Tsutsui's novel *Paprika* is told in two sections, Part 1 and Part 2.

I found Part 1 to be good, a gripping thriller that moved along to a breath-catching pause where the detective has just figured out the secret connection between Dr. Chiba and Paprika. Part 2 switches into office politics and academic powerplays as Vice President Inui, in the sudden absence of President Shima, seizes the presidency of the Institute and tries to discredit Chiba. While this represents an escalation of the conflict, the elevation makes it more cerebral and formalized, for me trading out the more visceral. Basically, the lines of battle between Chiba/Paprika and Inui are drawn at that point, and yet everybody goes to "work as usual" at the Institute during the day while they engage in dream/reality battles at night, almost in the style of comic book superheroes and supervillans.

I think that Kon took Part 1 as is and reworked Part 2 to make it more like Part 1. It seems to me that Kon uses Shakespeare's *A Midsummer Night's Dream* to do this. The book ends like the movie, with the marriage of Chiba (the dream machine agent) and Tokita (inventor of the dream machine), and in the movie this comes right after the surprising reveal that Chiba likes Tokita. In the book their affair is given early on—it is kept secret from others, but their main problem as a couple is that Tokita feels it is a "Beauty and the Beast" deal, with himself as the repulsive beast. He's the one who can't say "I love you" (the movie reverses this).

By shifting the structure, Kon turns the story into a courtship tale. Chiba/Paprika is the bride-to-be, but whom will she choose among potential suitors? One powerful man is in a wheelchair; one genial man is a dwarf; one creative man is morbidly obese; and the pretty-boy is her assistant. We the viewers are gulled into believing that the manly detective is her proper mate, and that Tokita is the "braying ass" of the play.

Kon makes additional refinements of merging or expansion. While the novel has a patient who dreams of movies, and there is another patient who is a detective, these two are combined in the film's detective. Tokita is obese in the book, but the other men are non-descript except for Osanai's exceptional good looks and the detective's action-hero physique: Kon makes Shima into a dwarf and turns Vice President Inui into the punningly wheelchair-bound "chairman."

In Tsutsui's novel, Reality takes a harder line: the Radio Club is a real bar, not an online/VR site; when Chiba becomes Paprika, we glimpse her putting on the fake freckles; in the dream world, Paprika doesn't do a lot of shapeshifting—when the film-dreamer casts her into a James Bond movie, she is "appalled" to see she looks like Ursula Andress (*Paprika*, 71).

On the other hand, some elements that might seem to have originated with Kon in fact come straight from the book: the Japanese doll, in small size and later giant form that smashes the ceiling glass of a real building (243); the action of reaching into a TV screen to pull someone to safety (326; 330) is like the use of TV as rapid transit in the movie; and waking up into another dream (Paprika uses it on Osanai the first time, but then the evil ones use it a couple times on her). The parade of international dolls in the movie marches from the desert toward reality, whereas in the book the hordes of Japanese dolls simply appear in the city like roving packs of goblins (315; 328).

The novel is more clear about the earliest manifestations of infectious insanity. When a Dr. Tsumura starts acting out, it is with a "Nazi salute" (12) from "a patient's paranoid delusions" (13). This patient-zero level symptom shows up again when Dr. Shima goes crazy (197; 206). (Kon's movie shows the Nazi salute among the dolls and the infected humans, but never names it as such.) The dolls come from a different source, from the victim Dr. Himuro. As the insanity infection spreads beyond these few cases, it becomes impossible to trace the sources of later images. At one point a giant Buddha appears and tramples a "trail of death and destruction" in the nightlife district (316). Dr. Tokita notes, "[T]hat parade of dolls and the giant Buddha . . . were obviously not from Inui's dreams" (328). Inui's images include "Lord Amon, a Marquis of Hell" (297), as well as a griffin (299), Glyro, "demonic manifestation of the child Jesus" (313), and Asmodai, "the demon of wrath and destruction" (314).

Still, the climax of the movie is almost entirely Kon (the book has no robot, no baby girl, no naked giant Inui, and the last battle happens in Sweden) except for the fact that the two guys from the bar play an important part. In the book, Inui isn't really setting out to conquer/control all dreams worldwide—his effective range is limited to just the area around Tokyo, and his main goal is revenge against Chiba and Tokita for winning the Nobel Prize (Inui had been in the running years earlier). So it is very personal and kind of petty, compared with the reality-shattering potential apocalypse of the film.

Some reviewers comment on how all the villains are gay. This detail is straight from the book, but even in the somewhat

simplified aspect of the film it is a bit more nuanced than reviewers let on: Inui "the chairman" is the main villain, and yes,
he's gay, but pretty-boy Osanai is patently bisexual (since he uses
his gay-fu with Inui and others, yet lusts after Chiba). In the
book Osanai uses gay-fu on Himuro to get access to the DC-Minis
(just like in the movie), but he also uses his uncanny metrosexual
powers on Nurse Sayama (115, 127) at the Institute so that on
short notice he can relieve his sexual tension after talking with
Chiba.

In the book, Inui tells Osanai to rape Chiba while he watches
over the DC-Mini (177); in the movie, Inui's "gay" interruption
helps to foil the rape. In the book, the first attempted rape is in
the real world, and Osanai punches Chiba into momentary uncon-
sciousness (182–83); the second one is in the dream world, and
Inui is there to help hold her down.

The beginning of Part 2 gives Inui's backstory, telling how in
Vienna he joined a society that follows "notions like Nietzsche's
Ubermensch" (210). Inui was profoundly shaped by studying art:

> *During his time at Vienna, he had visited art museums all
> over Europe . . . seen and admired numerous heretical or
> homosexual paintings, like Reni's* Martyrdom of St Sebas-
> tian . . . *Under their influence, he had developed a liking for
> beautiful youths with classical, Grecian looks. (211)*

These three passages form a coded reference to the controversial
Japanese author Yukio Mishima (1925–1970). Mishima celebrated
Nietzsche's *Ubermensch* in word and action. The painting mentioned in the quote, Reni's *Martyrdom of St. Sebastian,* is the same
one named by Mishima as a homoerotic touchstone in *Confessions
of a Mask* (1949), and Mishima celebrated classical Greek ideals of
beauty in word and action. Additionally, Mishima's fiction is noted
for its occasional sado-masochism, perhaps alluded to by Inui's
torture of Himuro and his plans to watch Chiba being raped; the
Nazi-salute bits of Tsutsui's novel might be a nod to Mishima's

play *My Friend Hitler* (1968), in one 1969 production of which, Mishima himself played the role of Adolf Hitler; and last, but perhaps most importantly, Mishima nearly won a Nobel Prize, another point he shares with the fictional Inui.

Through these points I hereby make the formal claim that Tsutsui's character Inui is based upon Yukio Mishima. Furthermore, Mishima's homosexuality is less significant than the traits of Nietzche-loving, Hitler-admiring, sadistic, and Nobel Prize-loser.

In any event, for Kon's movie adaptation the perception that "all the villains are gay" might be the perfect camouflage, the red herring to hide the reality that this film is an attack on a "god" of anime: the champion Hayao Miyazaki.

Book

Tsutsui, Yasutaka. *Paprika.* Translated by Andrew Driver. U.K.: Alma Books, 2009.

KON VERSUS MIYAZAKI

IN THIS CORNER...

I will now proceed to describe an artistic battle as if it really happened.

Andrew Osmond probes the unknown in this passage from *Satoshi Kon: The Illusionist* (2009),

> *Kon says he wasn't influenced by* Spirited Away *when he made* Paprika. *Indeed, he may not have seen Miyazaki's film, given that Kon is uninterested in anime as a medium. Miyazaki is indifferent too, so he may not have seen* Paprika; *one can only imagine the heckles if the directors were forced to watch each other's films. (112)*

While there is no confession that either auteur ever watched the work of the other, I take sardonic glee in the detail that Kon denies a connection between *Paprika* and *Spirited Away*, since I will argue the direct link between *Paprika* and the earlier Miyazaki movie *Princess Mononoke*.

For my purposes, I will write as if the two artists are engaged in direct combat, but it does not change much if they are blindly battling in generational warfare.

KON VS. MIYAZAKI: PAPRIKA

(2012; 2021)

Perhaps I'm the only one to see Kon's *Paprika* as a full-on attack against Miyazaki.

That final battle between the baby and the giant Inui (1:19:00–1:23:00) sums it up: a contest over "the world of dreams" or the field of anime, pitting a rising David against an established Goliath, with Kon as the David and Miyazaki as the Goliath.

In order to prepare the ground for this epic contest, the Miyazaki allusions in *Paprika* began much earlier.

First there is Chief Shima's "expansion" in the dream world, where he grows to tower over the trees until he "pops" (0:22:00). Despite the obvious Freudian play, this growth sequence evokes scenes from Miyazaki's *Princess Mononoke* where the smaller creature grows up into the giant Night Walker.

The next Miyazaki "nod" comes when the dolls below the throne of the dream parade do a twitching headshake movement (0:43:00), which is picked up again a few minutes later as Paprika encounters a lot of little Tokita dolls that make a whirring cicada sound while head twitching (0:49:00). This combination of twitch and sound forms an associational connection to the little forest spirits of *Princess Mononoke,* beings that make an otherworldly clicking sound when they rotate their heads, most notably when the giant Night Walker god is near.

The third thematic materialization follows quickly, since right after seeing the Tokita dolls, Paprika splits off her Tinker Bell mode, an image associated with Walt Disney, a chord played again a few minutes later when Paprika transforms into Pinocchio. In the novel, Paprika never becomes Tinker Bell, nor Pinocchio; these symbols of Disney apply to Miyazaki by association, as he is frequently termed "Japan's Walt Disney."

Trace echoes of *Princess Mononoke* and Walt Disney may seem small potatoes, but then comes a motherlode as Paprika/Tinker Bell discovers a vast Miyazaki-type tree. There is nothing in the book like this, where Chairman Inui is equated to a tree, but as noted before ("Four Miyazaki Points"), Miyazaki is famous for using giant trees in such differing films as the nostalgic *My Neighbor Totoro,* the steampunk *Castle in the Sky,* and the historical fantasy *Princess Mononoke.* In this case the tree is a thing of evil, having fed from Himuro so completely that the poor man is just an empty husk. Furthermore, this victim is found at the bottom of a shaft, exactly where the little sister Mei falls in *My Neighbor Totoro* when she meets Totoro himself. Paprika/Tinker Bell probes further, ultimately finding that the tree is Chairman Inui, who then uses his roots and branches like ropey appendages, trying to strike or grab the flying spy.

To pursue this line of thinking to an ugly end, we return to the Inui/Miyazaki tree, whose roots have drained the essence out of Himuro, pictured as a hollowed-out corpse (0:57:00). This is a good metaphor for the action of the story, but it could apply to Miyazaki in a disturbing way if Himuro is actually a mask for Yoshifumi Kondo, the protege director of Studio Ghibli's *Whisper of the Heart* (1995). A few years after the film was released, Kondo died of heart disease, said to be the result of overwork. He was only 47 years old.

.

Expanding this hypothetical war of Kon against Miyazaki

beyond the frame of *Paprika* reveals another bone of contention, another front: Nostalgia. Miyazaki favors nostalgia, as witnessed by many examples in his work. Kon is against nostalgia: for example, in the TV series *Paranoia Agent,* Kon shows nostalgia to be a trap when he has the older detective staying too long in the weird, two-dimensional town of the comfy past (episodes 11 and 13). In *Satoshi Kon: The Illusionist* (2009), Osmond addresses exactly this point and compares it to a Miyazaki work:

> *[Detective] Ikari's cutout utopia [of 1950s Japan] could also be a critique of nostalgic fantasies the world over: the boarding-school England in* Harry Potter, *or the gods-and-monsters Japanese heritage in* Spirited Away. *(100)*

Kon's earlier *Magnetic Rose* shows a different kind of nostalgia trap, where one artist's fixation on the past becomes a literal deathtrap for unsuspecting victims.

.

In the climactic battle scene of *Paprika,* the giant Chairman Inui seems a lot like an evil version of the Night Walker from Miyazaki's *Mononoke.* Both grow to giant size, both are semi-transparent, both are creatures of night. Granted, the Night Walker owes a lot to Godzilla, with its complex mix of good monster/bad monster, but now it is like we have stripped away the rubber suit to reveal a grumpy old man who rants against technology and hates humans.

Chairman Inui basically says he will become the emperor of dreams. Earlier, when Chiba asks him, "Do you plan to take over the world of dreams?" (0:53:44) he answers, "I am protecting them. I am the guardian of dreams." But now as a giant he says, "I can control the dreams, and even death! Now, to make the cosmos complete [. . .] I shall heal all deficiencies!" With a sweep of his arm he blasts an arc of real buildings, presumably causing an unknown amount of human death and maiming, to which Paprika says, "Way to go, Lord of Darkness!"

Despite all this build-up, the contest is almost anti-climactic:

Paprika goes inside the robot Tokita, where she presumably reunites with her Chiba-self.

Inui says, "The new cosmos begins with me!"

A baby girl emerges from the robot. She inhales the gale-force wind and grows into a toddler; she inhales the dream parade debris and grows into a child. Her identity is ambiguous: she might be the integration of Chiba and Paprika; but since her "superpower" of eating suggests Tokita, it seems more likely she is a daughter of Chiba/Paprika and Tokita.

Inui says, "Who is eating up my dream?"

Seeing the girl, he says, "Why won't you obey?"

He puts his hand on her head, to hold her down, to stop her growth.

She begins inhaling him, growing to womanhood as he diminishes, until he has vanished and she is full grown.

.

Having gone on record in 2010 as dubbing *Tokyo Godfathers* and *Paranoia Agent* as Kon's "Purgatory" and "Inferno" respectively ("Kon Explores the Insanity of Japan"), it is natural for me to declare *Paprika* as Kon's "Paradiso." *Pace* Osmond, who titles his *Paprika* chapter "Dream Goddess," the character Paprika is not a goddess: she is only a Beatrice-like guide. She defeats the Dark Lord but does not take his place; rather, like a lightning bolt that destroys a wolf tree whose vast shadow was starving out all the competition, she opens up the field for others to grow and thrive.

In terms of generational combat, Miyazaki's longevity and his Oscar-winning had bent the entire anime industry into the single vision of one man with his own generational fixations on nostalgia. Like Saturn, Miyazaki had "eaten" his own heir Yoshi-fumi Kondo; like a young Jupiter, Kon rises up to cut him down and free his siblings.

Book

Osmond, Andrew. *Satoshi Kon: The Illusionist*. Berkeley: Stone Bridge Press, 2009.

THE PATH TO PAPRIKA

(2021)

Satoshi Kon's path to *Paprika* is convoluted.

We will establish context, building a map for the path, by first identifying some films and books that had an early influence on Kon. For example, it appears that Kon's view of reality-bending and time-skipping come largely from the movie version of *Slaughterhouse-Five* (1972):

> *As far as Kurt Vonnegut is concerned, I only have read some of his works. The reason that I mention* Slaughterhouse-Five *as having the greatest influence, I saw the George Roy Hill-directed movie before I read the novel, and I was very much impressed how in the movie different places and times would be put together and expressed at the same time as we follow the protagonist. I have read the original novel itself, but it was the movie that left an impression on me and has had a huge influence on my work. (*TokyoPop, 2007)

This is noteworthy for revealing that Kon was drawn by the motion picture and, after reading the novel, became aware of the distinctive differences. Kon describes an identical set up with the film *Blade Runner* (1982):

As far as Philip K. Dick is concerned, I haven't read all of his works but I have read several. He is one of the authors that I prefer to read and it is also similar to the Kurt Vonnegut situation in that before I read the novel, I saw the movie Blade Runner. *I am very interested in the nightmare image. That is the influence I have from him which I have been saying. . . quite a bit in my interviews. Last year at the Hawaii Film Festival that was held, and the small synopsis they had in the program with* Paprika *said it was like a collision of Hello Kitty and Philip K. Dick. I felt that was correct.* (TokyoPop, 2007)

In contrast, when Kon tells a different interviewer about the Japanse science fiction author Yasutaka Tsutsui, it is text-based, rather than film-based:

Of course. I read a lot of his [Tsutsui's] books when I was in my early twenties, and years later when I began working in animation as a director and telling my own stories, I realized I had been influenced by him far more than I expected. (Midnight Eye, 2006)

Kon makes no mention of the visual adaptations made of Tsutsui's *The Girl Who Leapt Through Time* (1967), which was a television series in 1972 and motion pictures in 1983 and 1997, but perhaps this omission is due to those titles being unfamiliar outside of Japan.

This, then, is the context, the contours of the landscape. Now we begin the path.

Tsutsui's novel *Paprika* was serialized beginning in 1991, then published in book form in 1993. Kon presumably read it at this time, after having read Tsutsui's work for about ten years.

Focusing on Kon's line, "I realized I had been influenced by Tsutsui far more than I expected," I look to find traces of *Paprika* in

Kon's work prior to his making of *Paprika* itself.

Kon's role for *Magnetic Rose* (1995) was that of writer, not director; yet even so I see an approximation of *Paprika* in the fluid nature of reality as it is bent by Eva the diva. That is, the blurred line between dream and reality, which is central to Tsutsui's novel, is central here, too. Eva is the malignant form of the character Paprika, being a Siren who lures spacemen to their deaths in her arms.

Kon's *Perfect Blue* (1997) offers a second approximation of *Paprika*. While the film was based on a novel, Kon freely rewrote the material. This time the blurred line is between roles and real life; this time the actress Mima is the victim of a shadow-self, the monster, in an almost Jekyll-and-Hyde sort of way.

During the *Midnight Eye* interview, Kon tells about his first attempt to make a movie adaptation of *Paprika:*

> *In fact, after I finished making* Perfect Blue, *I considered making* Paprika *as my next film, not with Madhouse but with the producer who financed* Perfect Blue, *but that company (Rex Entertainment) unfortunately went bankrupt. But I did have the idea in my mind of making* Paprika *back in 1998.* (Midnight Eye, *2006*)

When Kon's first attempt at *Paprika* failed, he made *Millennium Actress* (2001) on commission for Madhouse, crafting a third approximation of *Paprika*. Here the *Slaughterhouse-Five* connection shines through, since Chiyoko ricochets through history like Vonnegut's hero Billy Pilgrim, yet Chiyoko shows a mastery of her power that makes her more like Paprika. The blurring is between history, history as depicted in films, roles, and personal histories.

Kon made *Tokyo Godfathers* (2003) and was working on *Paranoia Agent*. At the end of 2003 he met Tsutsui at an event sponsored by an anime magazine. Tsutsui, admiring Kon's work, personally gave him permission to make a movie based on *Paprika*. Looking back on this, Kon said,

> *"I was surprised. In 1998, I was looking for a project to take on. I actually considered* Paprika *even though I thought that it would be tough to adapt. A few years later the author asks me about adapting it into a film. It had to be destiny. That's what I told myself, anyway."* ("Tsutsui and Kon's Paprika," *03:55–04:26*)

Kon had dreamed of this goal for years, perhaps as many as ten years. He had worked toward it, honing his craft, and suddenly it dropped into his hands.

According to my reasoning, Kon at this stage had three approximations of the character Paprika: Eva (the Siren), Mima (the Victim), and Chiyoko (the Chaser). It is interesting to consider how each contributed to the character Paprika and her world in Kon's final feature film.

Sources
Interview by Jason Gray for *Midnight Eye,* November 2006.

Interview by Bill Aguiar for *TokyoPop,* April 2007.

"Tsutsui and Kon's *Paprika,*" featurette on *Paprika* DVD, 2007.

THE WIND RISES: TWO TEXTS INTO ONE FILM

(2021)

Miyazaki's *The Wind Rises* (2013) is a blend of two unrelated sources: one being the biography of the man who invented the Mitsubishi Zero, and the other a novel about a man who marries a woman with tuberculosis.

The majority of the film, dealing with the struggles of an aeronautical engineer, comes straight from the life of Jiro Horikoshi. Decades after inventing the Mitsubishi Zero, Horikoshi wrote a book about the process, *Eagles of Mitsubishi: the Story of the Zero Fighter* (1970, English translation 1981), a text containing a few autobiographical bits that Miyazaki seems to have used.

Horikoshi, describing his childhood in Gunma prefecture, writes:

> *In my sleep I would often dream of flying in a small airplane of my own construction, high over fields and rivers or sometimes close to the ground. (9)*

This seems a perfect blueprint for the opening of the Miyazaki movie.

Regarding Horikoshi going away to college in Tokyo, he writes: "I began my studies in April 1923" (9). He does not mention the Kanto earthquake of September 1923, nor the subsequent fire at the university library, but it is a fact that the Imperial University Library lost around 700,000 volumes to the flames, so Miyazaki has a basis for including scenes of the library fire.

After graduating, Horikoshi went to work designing airplanes at Mitsubishi. He writes about the work strain affecting his health:

> *During this time, I was involved in finishing the study concerning Commander Shimokawa's accident . . . my health became so bad that my doctor recommended I take a rest. (121)*

Under medical advice, he rests.

> *I spent the month of October very quietly at my birthplace in Gunma prefecture. (121–22)*

Some pages later, the problem comes again.

> *Shortly after returning to work, I had to take some additional leave . . . I took rest at a relative's home in Kamakura from about the end of 1941 until late February 1942 . . . I spent each day . . . walking during the day and sleeping deeply at night just as I had done in November when staying at my hometown. (129)*

Horikoshi describes a medical leave time spent in Gunma and another at Kamakura. The first one, being shortly after a plane accident, seems similar to the situation in the movie where the hero, stressed by an aircraft failure, goes to recuperate at a health spa in the mountains. While Miyazaki changes the venue from "staying with relatives" to "resting at a health resort," there is a strong basis in Horikoshi's life story; in fact, Miyazaki is probably downplaying this aspect, since in the movie all health sympathies are focused on the fictional wife.

For his movie Miyazaki used the airplane development time-line, but he also incorporated details from Horikoshi's private life, including his childhood flying dreams and the heavy toll on his health from his work at designing planes.

Miyazaki's source for the movie title and most of the details about the fictional woman is Tatsuo Hori's *The Wind Rises* (1937). (In real life, Horikoshi's wife was not terminally ill at a young age; and when Horikoshi died of pneumonia in 1982 at the age of 78, he was survived by five children, another difference from the childless hero of the movie.) Miyazaki uses Hori's novel to provide an emotional counterbalance to the engineer's more cerebral struggle.

Set in Japan during the 1930s, Hori's novel begins with a sudden gust blowing a painting off its easel onto the ground. This prompts the narrator to quote the title line "The wind rises, we must try to live" to his girlfriend the artist. She stands up and re-trieves the canvas. Discovering that it now has leaves stuck to the wet paint, she says, "Oh dear! What if my father sees this?"

Miyazaki breaks up this opening into three separate scenes: the couple first share the French poetry quote while on a train, just before the Kanto earthquake; years later, when Jiro goes to the mountain hotel, he sees a young woman painting, whereupon the wind blows her parasol so that Jiro must catch it (1:04:00–1:06:00); on another day the two are caught in a storm that ruins her artwork, and then they meet her father (1:11:00).

In the novel the nameless narrator is a poet who has deeply studied such European poets as Paul Valéry (1871–1945) and Rainer Maria Rilke (1875–1926). The phrase "The wind rises, we must try to live" comes from a Valéry poem "The Graveyard by the Sea," within which the sense of the quoted phrase is that, even though we are surrounded by death, we must reject despair. Hori's novel follows through on this: the poet marries the girlfriend, knowing she has TB; he stays with her at the sanitorium until she dies in December, 1936; and in the final section, "The Valley of the

Shadow of Death," it is December 1937 when he seeks solace in Christianity before finding hope in the sound of the wind.

Miyazaki artfully blends his two source texts: the inventor hero meets his future wife at a health spa where he is trying to shake off work stress and she is trying to beat TB. Romantically, Miyazaki shows how they had met years earlier and shared the title phrase at that time. In the movie's end, Miyazaki translates "The Valley of the Shadow of Death" from Hori's novel into a graveyard of airplanes where the wind of life still blows, however softly.

Book
Horikoshi, Jiro. *Eagles of Mitsubishi: the Story of the Zero Fighter*. Seattle: University of Washington Press, 1981.

MIYAZAKI VS. KON:
THE WIND RISES

(2021)

The Wind Rises (2013), said to be Miyazaki's final film, is received by critics as being quite different from all his other movies.

·

The Christian Science Monitor "His movie is visually as beautiful as anything he's ever done. Conceptually, it's muddled. The collision between poetic fancifulness and grim reality, between peace and war, never falls into focus. Miyazaki has seized on a great theme only to soft-pedal it."

Empire "While Miyazaki's two-hour-long, historical-melodrama swansong is destined to be his most divisive film yet, it is also his most adult and interesting, and never less than visually breathtaking throughout."

RogerEbert.com "*Wind* is both benign and ominous."

Dissolve "While the film's individual moments and images are often fantastically wrought, the story elements often seem as unintegrated as the moral exegesis."

St. Louis Post-Dispatch "Typically lovely to look at, with big-eyed young people espousing high ideals amid natural splendor. But outside of their bubble, a prickly history looms, and Miyazaki's dubious attitude toward the wartime role of his hero makes the movie a mixed blessing."

Time Out "Jiro's genius is godlike, but his personality is nonexistent; time is too-briskly spanned, then ground into blow-by-blow melodrama."

•

The above quotes say *The Wind Rises* is "muddled," "divisive," "ominous," and something like "morally questionable."

I agree that it is muddled, divisive, ominous, and morally questionable. Within the Miyazaki catalogue, *The Wind Rises* bears comparison to *Princess Mononoke,* since both movies posit a technology god. One obvious difference is that *Wind*'s Jiro sees no competition for technology, whereas Lady Eboshi is well aware and goes hunting the forest god. And while the forest god gives both death and life, the technology god gives only death.

Furthermore, Lady Eboshi makes an important switch at the end of her film. It might be abrupt and vague, but she clearly signals, "Well, that didn't work. Let's try something different." Jiro makes no such change, even though he has an Italian spirit guide who says the right things. While the guide does not offer any solution, he at least outlines the problem that Flying Technology is a Siren, a two-faced, lying, murderous god with no goodness at all. This proves why religious competition is not really necessary, since the guide can describe the problem, and all one has to do is stop worshipping that death god.

Jiro only nods. He never weeps. He never sighs. He never expresses the guide's imparted wisdom using his own words. In ancient Greek drama, that's a failing grade.

While some attribute the unusual nature of this film to Miyazaki having a loss of power, I see it as Miyazaki responding to the challenges posed by the work of Satoshi Kon.

•

The Wind Rises shows signs of conflict with Miyazaki tropes. Revisiting my 2005 piece on "Four Miyazaki Points" to apply its model of "Flight," "Technology versus Magic," "The Miyazaki Heroine," and "The Miyazaki Tree" to *The Wind Rises* will make it plain.

Flight: In *The Wind Rises,* flight is dangerous! During the aircraft development stage, planes disintegrate, test pilots die; but when planes are released, they do nothing but kill. There is nothing positive about flight; which amounts to a complete refutation of Miyazaki's lifelong romance with airplanes.

Technology versus Magic: In *The Wind Rises,* this is changed into "Reality versus Dream."

The Miyazaki Heroine: *The Wind Rises* lacks a Miyazaki Heroine.

The Miyazaki Tree: *The Wind Rises* lacks a Miyazaki Tree.

In addition to these big changes to the standard Miyazaki mode, *The Wind Rises* shows signs of homage to Satoshi Kon: Reality versus Dream; the use of the Kanto Earthquake; and a number of elements from *Millennium Actress.*

"Reality versus Dream" is common to Kon but alien to Miyazaki, for whom the place of wonder is always a different time and/or a different place. Even *Spirited Away* has a transition from the real contemporary world to the spirit world.

The "kingdom of dreams" in particular seems like a direct response to Kon's "world of dreams" at the end of *Paprika.* Early in Miyazaki's film, the Italian aeronautical engineer Caproni says, "This world is a dream. Welcome to my kingdom" (0:09:20). Where Chairman Inui acts like a tyrant, Caproni acts as a guide or mentor. At the movie's midpoint, Caproni invites Jiro to attend his last flight (0:55:00), a time when Jiro is taller than the Italian. At the end, looking over the wreckage of planes, Caproni says, "Our kingdom of dreams" (1:59:00). In Miyazaki's version, the king nurtures his heir, even though the kingdom itself is horribly flawed by human imperfections.

In *The Wind Rises,* Miyazaki presses into Kon's home territory, perhaps becoming "more Kon" than Kon himself in blurring transitions between Reality and Dream. There are cases where Jiro is not even sleeping when he talks to Caproni: under the stress of carrying a wounded woman, Jiro has a vision of Italian bombers flying over a burning city (0:19:00); under the strain of fighting the library fire, Jiro responds to Caproni (0:24:24). There are times when there are no transitions: when Jiro is in Germany there is no transition to his walking in the snow toward a stopped train while a burning Japanese bomber falls (0:53:05); likewise, there is no transition to the dream of war, with Japan in flames, wreckage of planes, and serene Caproni on the hill (1:59:00). Building upon the two transitionless examples, there are cases where reality comes into question because of abrupt shifts: at the hotel in the Japanese mountains, the German tourist disappears so abruptly it suggests he is not real (1:16:00), yet later the German is pursued by the Japanese Thought Police, suggesting he is real.

Another detail is the notion that "artists have ten years of creativity," as stated twice by Caproni, once at the beginning of the movie, and once at the end. On the surface this idea reflects sentiments expressed by Miyazaki himself over the years, while it maps to the real-life experience of the aeronautical engineer between his design of the Mitsubishi warplanes IMF10 and Zero. Poignantly, though, it also matches the nine years of Kon's life from *Perfect Blue* (1997) to *Paprika* (2006).

A second homage to Kon is in the use of the Kanto Earthquake, and then the two-year recovery. Miyazaki often uses disguised mushroom clouds in his work: *Nausicaä of the Valley of the Wind* has a "god warriors" apocalypse in the background and threat of repeat at the end; *Porco Rosso* uses World War One as a more recent apocalypse; and for *Howl's Moving Castle*, a steampunk apocalypse storms in out of nowhere. For Miyazaki, Nature is good, Humanity is evil. Humanity is destroying Nature. Miyazaki's use of the Kanto earthquake in *The Wind Rises* shows Nature being far more destructive, which makes it unique among Miyazaki's films, but the Kanto earthquake is also a famous signature of Kon's *Millennium Actress,* where earthquakes mark significant points of the film, and the Kanto quake signals the heroine's birth. Then there is the "two years to recover" bit. In *The Wind Rises,* Jiro's sister visits Tokyo two years after the quake and says, "I never dreamed Tokyo would recover so quickly" (0:29:30). In Kon's *Paranoia Agent,* Tokyo is destroyed for the season finale, after which the screen fades to black, but then appears a new scene of towering buildings, with radio commentary stating that, after two years of work, the reconstruction of Tokyo is officially complete.

The homage draws upon Kon's *Millennium Actress* in the use of a Landscape Painter; the presence of the Japanese Thought Police; a vision of Japan in flames; and in presenting the scale of an entire life.

While Hori's novel *The Wind Rises* has a landscape painter as a love interest, Kon's *Millennium Actress* does too, and Chiyoko meets him early in the film, an encounter that shapes her life along with the rest of the movie. The image of the artist at his easel in a landscape recurs throughout *Millennium Actress,* as well as the easel by itself in a landscape. When Miyazaki depicts Jiro finding the unattended easel in a grove (1:10:00), it seems therefore a tribute to Kon.

The cameo appearance of the Japanese Thought Police in *The Wind Rises,* investigating first the German tourist and then the hero Jiro, seems an homage to *Millennium Actress* where the Thought Police play a central role.

A third homage to *Millennium Actress* is in the image of Japan in flames, and the ruins of planes. At the end of *The Wind Rises,* Jiro sees Japan suffering defeat, an image unique within Miyazaki's films, but one that echoes the firebombing of Tokyo scene in *Millennium Actress.*

Then there is the scale of an entire life within a movie, which is established at the beginning of *Millennium Actress* and revealed to be the case at the end of *The Wind Rises.*

Beyond the homage to Kon on such specific points, *The Wind Rises* shows signs of responding to Kon's more general charges regarding Japan's "undigested past" through: the use of anti-nostalgia; an acknowledgement of Japanese blame; and an addressing of Japan's collective amnesia.

Miyazaki's trademark nostalgia is changed into anti-nostalgia at several points in the film. As Jiro's train is approaching Nagoya, he sees a crowd of men alongside the railroad, men desperately looking for work (0:30:46). At Nagoya, he witnesses people mobbing a bank that has failed (0:31:52). One late night, after working on a new design, he offers cake to waiting children, but they run away (0:42:40). This is followed by a shot of a hobo campfire under the train bridge.

Miyazaki acknowledges Japanese blame. This is in contrast to *Nausicaä,* where the apocalypse is an ancient curse of a previous civilization; *Porco Rosso,* where the apocalypse of World War One was years ago in Europe; and *Howl's Moving Castle,* where the apocalypse is in fairyland. But in *The Wind Rises,* Japan is the aggressor, pushing into China; and the main character is designing the Zero, the most famous Japanese warplane. This is a bold move by Miyazaki: Kon keeps his *Millennium Actress* heroine a step removed, making her a girl who falls in love with an anti-imperialist agent. Even Kobayashi's Human Condition trilogy uses a socialist as its hero. Kon and Kobayashi use main characters who are swept up by events, figures who are shaped by the war rather than shaping the war, as Jiro does.

Miyazaki even spells out Japan's "collective amnesia" in a direct and forceful way. In *The Wind Rises,* the German tourist tells Jiro four milestones of Japan's bad behavior, a laundry list Jiro already knows:

> *"Start a war in China, then forget it. Make a puppet state in Manchuria, then forget it. Quit the League of Nations, then forget it. Make the world your enemy, then forget it. Japan will blow up. Germany will blow up, too." (1:15:00)*

The "start a war in China" line probably refers to the Mukden incident (1931), an event that Japan used as an excuse to separate Manchuria from China. When Japan made Manchuria a puppet state in 1932, the League of Nations objected to this, so Japan quit the League in 1933.

The Wind Rises is a difficult film in Miyazaki's catalogue but I find a new appreciation for it in seeing it as a response to Satoshi Kon. Miyazaki pays homage to Kon's work, *Millennium Actress* in particular, and grapples bravely with Japan's "undigested past."

But the reader might say, "No, Miyazaki is not acknowledging anything. Jiro does not have a big epiphany at the end, something like, *My beautiful machine made possible the sneak attack on Pearl Harbor and the suicidal attacks of the kamikaze pilots. The god of flying technology lures us with a beautiful vision but only delivers death, doom, and destruction.*"

Perhaps Miyazaki cannot do that because it is not historically accurate.

Or maybe he wants all of that to happen inside of the audience.

APPENDIX: SATOSHI KON TIMELINE

1984: manga "Toriko-Prisoner"

1985: manga "Carve"

1986: manga "Horseplay," "Baseball Brats," "Summer of Anxiety," and "Focus"

1987: manga "Day has Dawned," "Kidnappers," and "Guests"

1988: manga "Waira," "Picnic," and "Beyond the Sun"

1989: manga "Joyful Bell," "The Desert Dolphin," and "The Adventures of Master Basho"

1990: long-form manga *Tropic of the Sea*

1991: live-action motion picture *World Apartment Horror* (Kon as writer); manga "World Apartment Horror"; anime feature *Roujin Z* (Kon as art director and set designer)

1994: long-form manga *Seraphim: 266613336 Wings* begins

1995: film "Magnetic Rose" segment of *Memories* anthology;

begins long-form manga *Opus,* ends long-form manga *Seraphim* without completion

1996: ends long-form manga *Opus* without completion

1997: *Perfect Blue*

2001: *Millennium Actress*

2003: *Tokyo Godfathers*

2004: *Paranoia Agent*

2006: *Paprika*

2008: short anime "Good Morning" for *Ani*Kuri15*

2010: Satoshi Kon dies of pancreatic cancer.

APPENDIX: MANGA BY KON

An annotated list of Satoshi Kon's work in manga from 1984 to 1996.

·

Dream Fossil (2015), a collection of fifteen short manga stories from the 1980s.

1. "Carve" (1985). Post-apocalyptic Japan where Espers have been cast out by Normals, such that the Espers live in the city ruins. Esper Kei, who carves wood, and his girlfriend Ann. She has slight telekinetic powers, trying to lift a cigarette but dropping it; he can lift the cigarette easily.

Kei is kidnapped by police in a medical/military program where Espers are being changed into large robots to attack the Espers. When the attack comes, Ann believes Kei is still in one and it proves her right by shaping an image of her face out of debris before dying.

2. "Horseplay" (1986). A private high school baseball team is thrust into championship when another team has to bow out due to scandal. Emphasis on how morally bad the first-string baseball players are: smoking, drinking, and a pornography collection including a doll. Ippei is the younger good guy tasked with keeping star Goro in line. This strict shepherding improves Goro's play but keeps him on edge. Rivalry between the baseball team and the soccer team turns into chaotic battle royale with a surprising twist at the end, in that humble good guys win out of nowhere.

3. "Baseball Brats" (1986). Young students play, practice, play.

A case where the player on one team helps out a neglected player on the other team by giving him a perfect pitch.

4. "Summer of Anxiety" (1986). Two high school senior buddies ride bicycles to the beach on their last summer vacation. They get separated but find each other in time to help with a fistfight against bullies.

5. "Focus" (1986). A middle school boy's private tutor is tasked with trailing the boy from school to home for a week. Tutor discovers boy meeting with a high school girl, who is the daughter of his homeroom teacher. But the twist in the end is that the students are not having an affair, her father is having one with his mother.

6. "Day has Dawned" (1987). Three high school seniors waiting on their college acceptance letters go out to Soapland. All their friendship tensions come to the fore.

7. "Kidnappers" (1987). A car thief takes an idling minivan as opportunistic crime, but then discovers a kidnapped child in the back. But the kidnapper won't give up. Chase sequences anticipate action scenes in *Tokyo Godfathers*, specifically the "Door of moving mini-van" stunt (192), and the "Kick off from vehicle about to plow into storefront" stunt (193–94).

8. "Guests" (1987). Family of four moves into house from apartment. Big brother sees ghost. One by one the others see ghosts, too, but the parents are in denial. The father places an amulet which seems to help for the housewarming party, but in fact the situation gets worse and ghosts explode into the party. It turns out the house is located on a spirit pathway and the awkward placement of the amulet caused the traffic to build up.

9. "Waira" (1988). Samurai warfare, with a lord being hunted in a rebel insurrection led by his brother-in-law. The lord and his few retainers slip away from a bad situation. Things get supernatural with "Waira," a specter of the mountain that horribly murders many soldiers on both sides. Turns out to be a tiger. In a surprising twist, the lord manages to win against all odds, and he gives clemency to his brother-in-law.

10. "Picnic" (1988). Science fiction. A couple goes exploring

the drowned ruins of their former home town.

11. "Beyond the Sun" (1988). Family of four visits grandma at her mountain hospital, then they go to the nearby beach. Grandma ends up on a runaway gurney that takes her to the beach, too. Anticipates action sequences of *Tokyo Godfathers.* The feature *Roujin Z* (1991) is similar for having an elderly bed-ridden patient who goes upon an unexpected, action-filled trip down to the beach, all in his automated hospital bed. *Roujin Z* was Kon's first anime job, but he was art director and set designer rather than a screenwriter.

12. "Joyful Bell" (1989). A Christmas story of a Tokyo guy with the Santa job who finds a lost little girl who asks him for a father. They go on a trek across town to return her to her mother, but she runs ahead at the apartment building and disappears. He meets his estranged wife and they agree not to get the divorce after all. Having made this agreement, she reveals she is pregnant. Anticipates *Tokyo Godfathers* in a number of ways: Christmas time adventure comedy; helping a lost child; an episodic journey across the big city; and benevolent supernatural elements.

13. "The Desert Dolphin" (1989). A weird war story in 1942. Somehow separated from their company, two German soldiers in a tank search for water and supplies in North Africa.

14. "The Adventures of Master Basho" (1989). A two-page comedy ending in haiku. The haiku aspect is picked up later in *Tokyo Godfathers* as a habit of the character Hana.

15. "Toriko–Prisoner" (unpublished award-winner, 1984). In a world of robot cops, a juvenile delinquent is sent to "rehab" at "The Center."

Tropic of the Sea (1990), Kon's first long-form manga.

In a contemporary seaside town, the protagonist Yosuke's father is head priest at a shrine which has a mermaid's egg. The promise was to tend the egg for 60 years and then return it to the sea, then take charge of the next egg, in exchange for calm seas and bountiful catches of fish. But now the town wants to build a resort, and the old ways are under threat.

World Apartment Horror (1991), anthology of four supernatural stories, including three earlier pieces.

    1. "World Apartment Horror" (written by Katsuhiro Otomo). This is the manga adaptation of the live-action 1991 movie of the same name, directed by Otomo, from a story by Kon. A yakuza member is sent to fix problems at a Tokyo apartment full of foreigners, but he encounters malignant spirits and hellish scenes.

    2. "Guests" (1987), collected later in *Dream Fossil*.

    3. "Waira" (1988), collected later in *Dream Fossil*.

    4. "Joyful Bell" (1989), collected later in *Dream Fossil*.

Seraphim: 266613336 Wings (1994–95), an incomplete long-form manga written by Mamoru Oshii and drawn by Satoshi Kon.

    From the back cover:

Two of Anime's Greatest Directors Once Made a Manga Together

An unfinished collaboration between Ghost in the Shell's *Mamoru Oshii and* Paprika's *Satoshi Kon,* Seraphim: 266613336 Wings *is a dark journey into a world ravaged by a pandemic that induces apocalyptic visions in the mind, and twists the bodies of men into the corpses of angels. Amid the dying cities sealed off to their fate, three twenty-first-century Magi accompany a mysterious young girl in search of a revelation. But when medicine has become a cult, are they here to kill or to cure [. . .] and is this angel plague a withered branch on the tree of life, or a new birthing of existence?*

In his afterword to the English-language edition, Carl Gustav Horn writes:

Despite the creative conflicts [between Kon and Oshii] to

which Watanabe alludes, and Kon's referring to Seraphim *as his "bastard child," Kon might very well have had some lingering affection for the traditions behind* Seraphim; *it certainly seems worth remarking that his 2003 film* Tokyo Godfathers *takes inspiration from John Ford's 1948 movie* 3 Godfathers, *and of course both took inspiration from the story of the Magi. (263)*

Seraphim reveals that Kon was working on a "three Magi" story some years prior to *Tokyo Godfathers.* In *Seraphim,* Oshii's Magi even have the traditional names of Melchior, Balthazar, and Caspar, here assigned to a man with a dark reputation for destroying countries; another man who is openly fond of the Gaia "heresy"; and a beagle. Then there is "Sera," the mysterious girl the three Magi must escort into the heart of Eurasia.

Opus (1995–96). Kon's last long-form manga, left unfinished in 1996 because Kon's anime directorial career took off.

Metafictional, it is the story of Espers fighting evil, but it is also about the manga creator struggling with the characters he has created. As such it has links to the reality-blurring aspects of Kon's films, especially *Millennium Actress* and *Paprika,* where transitions between states become more pronounced.

Books
Kon, Satoshi. *Dream Fossil.* Vertical, 2015.
———. *Tropic of the Sea.* Vertical, 2013.
———. *World Apartment Horror.* (No English translation.)
———. *Opus.* Dark Horse, 2014.

Oshii, Mamoru (author) and Satoshi Kon (illustrator). *Seraphim: 266613336 Wings.* Dark Horse Manga, 2015.

INDEX

PUBLISHING HISTORY

Anime review of feature *Howl's Moving Castle* (dir. Hayao Miyazaki), *The Internet Review of Science Fiction* (Vol. II, No. 7), Aug 2005.

"Satoshi Kon Explores the Insanity of Japan" [Kon's *Paranoia Agent* and *Millennium Actress* seen through the lens of van Wolferen's *The Enigma of Japanese Power*], *The Internet Review of Science Fiction*, Feb 2010.

Anime review of feature *Paprika* (dir. Satoshi Kon), *The Internet Review of Science Fiction*, Aug 2008.

BOOKS BY THIS AUTHOR

True Sf Anime

Can someone love anime while hating transforming mecha robots? Is there a world of Japanese animation beyond giant bubble-filled eyes and predictable plots?

In this book of essays, Michael Andre-Driussi explores dozens of rare gems of anime, all built in the "true SF" tradition: movies and TV shows with real stories, real characters, and real explorations of the technological possibilities of the future. The works covered include "Paprika," "Planetes," "Wings of Honneamise," "The Melancholy of Haruhi Suzumiya," and more.

Roadside Picnic Revisited: Seven Articles On The Soviet Novel That Inspired The Film "Stalker"

A collection of essays and a book review relating to "Roadside Picnic," the Soviet science fiction novel by Arkady and Boris Strugatsky. The subject is the novel, and there is nothing about the movie beyond a brief mention.

Topics include:
*Close reading of the novel to unlock its mysteries.
*Translation triumphs and errors.
*A British novel that had a profound influence on "Roadside Picnic."
*The critical reception of "Roadside Picnic" in the West.
*The original plan for "Roadside Picnic" and the terrible com-

promise that came.

Fallout Stories

A celebration of "Fallout," as both concept and video game, with nine post-apocalyptic stories, two articles on "Fallout 3," and a List of Ten Classic Tales in the Style of "Fallout."

The stories span a spectrum, the first three being gritty realism, but after that things get more fantastic, with robots, zombies, and the like.

9 7 8 1 9 4 7 6 1 4 2 5 3